PHILIP THE ARAB
A Study in Prejudice

Philip the Arab
A Study in Prejudice

Stacey International
128 Kensington Church Street
London W8 4BH
Tel: 020 7221 7166; Fax: 020 7792 9288
E-mail: stacey.international@virgin.net

© Yasmine Zahran 2001

ISBN: 1 900988 283

Edited by Jonathan Tubb
Designed by Kitty Carruthers

All rights reserved. No part of this publication may be reproduced, stored in a retrieval system or transmitted in any form or by any means, electronic, mechanical, photographic or otherwise, without prior permission of the copyright owner.

British Library Cataloguing-in-Publication Data
A catalogue record for this publication is available from the British Library

Printed and bound in the UK

PHILIP THE ARAB
A Study in Prejudice

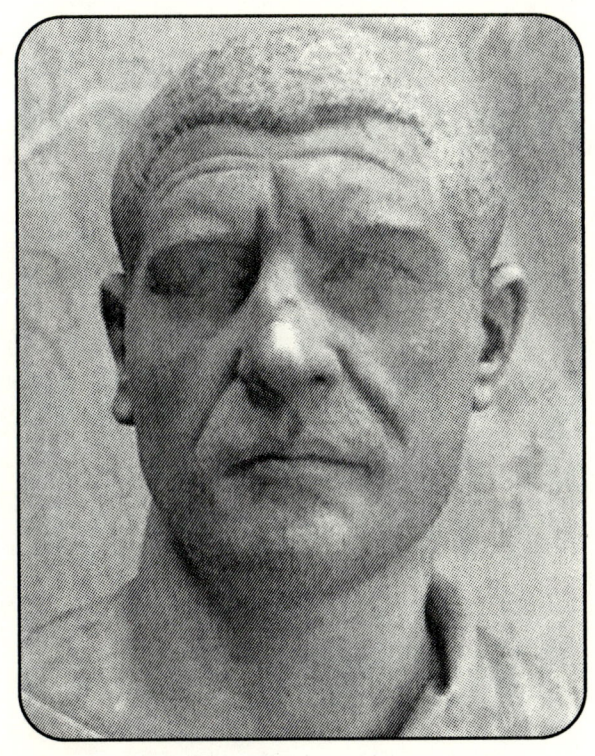

Yasmine Zahran

To
Philip the Arab

son of a sheikh, Roman Emperor and philhellene

"Ταὐτγς τοι γενής τε και αἵματος εὔχομαι εἴναι."

I boast that I am of your race and blood.
The Illiad VI, 211

CONTENTS

Foreword	6
Preface - Speak Otacilia, Speak	7
Introduction	11
Chapter One: Denigration and Prejudice	17
Chapter Two: Arabs Beyond Arabia	23
Chapter Three: The Hauran	39
Chapter Four: War and Prejudice	49
Chaper Five: Arabia Revisited	69
Chapter Six: Emperor in Rome	87
Chapter Seven: The First Christian Emperor	105
Chapter Eight: Sic Transit Gloria	119
Epilogue:	131
Notes:	135
Main Sources	149

FOREWORD

Marcus Julius Philippus was born in the village of Shahba in the Hauran - the black basaltic region of southern Syria. Little is known of his early life or career: he first rose to prominence during Gordian III's Parthian campaign of AD 243 when, as an equestrian officer, he succeeded the influential Timesitheus as Praetorian Prefect. On the death of Gordian himself the following year, Philip was proclaimed Emperor by the army. Abandoning the Parthian war, he returned to Rome, and in 246 fought successful campaigns on the Danube. In 247 he made his son, Philip II, Augustus and in 248 he celebrated the last Secular Games held in Rome. Philip died in 249 at the hands of Decius, a soldier entrusted with the task of securing the Danubian frontier, and whose successes led to his usurping the throne. His son, Philip II, was murdered by the Praetorian Guard.

This brief summary, although factually accurate, says little of Philip the man - his character, his aspirations or his vision. He remains for many, a figure surrounded by mystery and controversy. In this fascinating and well-researched book, Yasmine Zahran explores every aspect of Philip's life and achievements. She examines his alleged complicity in the death of Gordian III, and reveals a conspiracy of defamation, based on prejudice – directed not only at Philip's ethnicity as an Arab, but also at his religion as a Christian. By this means she explains the tensions in his life, as with the need to revere his background through the building of Philippopolis at his home village of Shahba, whilst at the same time appealing to Rome as a citizen emperor.

Through this sensitive study, Philip the Arab emerges as one of the most interesting figures of the turbulent third century.

Jonathan N. Tubb

Preface
Speak, Speak Otacilia

The night was heavy, a storm was raging outside and I, a lover of storms, listened with awe to the howling wind and hissing rain until the storm slowly abated. But sleep eluded me, and I picked up a book from my night table, an old edition of Gibbon's Decline and Fall. I opened it at random, with great expectations – for I believe in omens – and my eyes fell on 'Philip the Arab'. I read a few lines and must have fallen asleep with the book open. Suddenly I saw a figure standing near the open door, a handsome man with an air of majesty and a gaze so intense it seemed he was looking through me and beyond. I noted his slightly aquiline nose and his close-cropped hair. He walked towards me and, pointing to his right, said, 'Speak, speak, Otacilia.' I did not know what language he spoke, but I understood and followed his gaze, to distinguish the figure of a woman beside him, with a bent back and dishevelled hair, her hands furtively searching the floor. In a flash I remembered that Otacilia Severa was the empress and wife of Philip the Arab. The man before me was the emperor himself!

He spoke to me. 'I cannot communicate with her. She spends all her days looking in the fields of Borea for the fragments of my body, my decapitated head. But she cannot find them and she cannot rest nor give me rest. She has become mute although I plead with her to speak. She retrieved the mutilated body of Philippus, our son, after the praetorians tore him from her breast and stabbed him before her eyes. She buried him, and then was secretly carried away by my faithful old valet from Rome to Borea to hunt for my body.

'Tell her to speak,' he pleaded. 'She must tell the Romans what happened. She must tell them of the betrayal and treachery. . .' His voice faded, and the last words were almost inaudible. 'She must tell the truth.'

I woke in a cold sweat, with a prevailing sense of loss, of sadness and of grief.

Rising from my bed, I hunted through my shelves for something on third century Roman history. I read bits and pieces and was amazed. Philip was dismissed in a few words; accused of poisoning and murder, he was dragged through the mud and treacherously killed.

The next day I called a friend, a professor of Arabic literature, and asked him to find Arabic sources on Philip. In a few days he came back and said, 'I have bad news for you: there are very few Arabic sources on Philip. I only found three, all written around a thousand years after his death.' Bad news indeed, but his next words gave me a jolt. 'He came to see me last

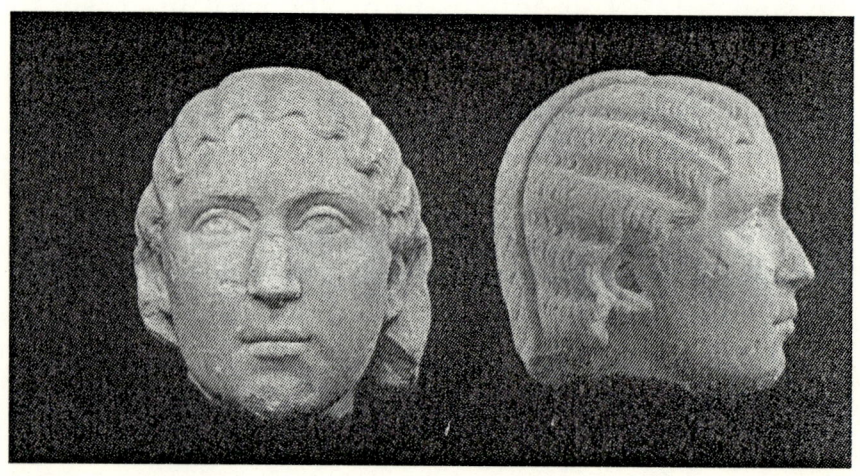

night,' he said. 'He must have known I was searching for him because he stood at the door and said nothing. "Who are you?" I said. He answered, "I am Philip the Arab. Otacilia is mute and I want you to tell [and here he mentioned my name] to speak, tell her to speak." And with that he vanished.'

"What language did he speak?' I asked him.

'Arabic, of course!'

I told him about my dream. 'Well, that's that,' my friend replied, 'Philip wants you to speak.'

'Why me?' I asked. My friend hesitated. 'He must be very canny, he knows your morbid passion for lost causes. Or he knows, perhaps, that you live in the past, which you are always seeking to evoke.'

For three years following that dream I searched for Philip. Now it is time to speak, and here I offer what I have discovered. I keep hoping Philip will return some stormy night, to tell me if he approves, and I pray that I have given the spectre of Otacilia repose from searching the earth to gather his remains. . . And I wonder if the truth, extracted from the many layers of distortion, misconception and prejudice, has finally laid their shades to rest.

The marble portrait (*far left*), from the Kircheriano Museum is presumed to be of Otacilia, wife of Philip the Arab, from its likeness to her image on the coin (*left*) minted in AD 247/248.

Marble bust of Philip the Arab wearing a laurel wreath.

INTRODUCTION

THE ARRIVAL of Marcus Julius Verus Philippus, Imperatur Caesar, Pius, Felix Invictus Augustus, Persicus, Parthicus, Carpicus and Germanicus Maximus – known as Philip the Arab – on the throne of the Caesars was a momentous event in pre-Islamic Arab history. An Arab from a peripheral tribe outside the Arabian peninsula, he became the master of Rome. He ruled almost four centuries before another Arab, from within Arabia proper, the Prophet Mohammad, raised the banner of Islam.

Philip the Arab was born as he was to die – in the eye of a storm, a storm created by the assassination of Alexander Severus and his imperial mother, Mamaea, at Mayence in AD 235. The Severan dynasty marked the height of Roman power, and was followed by half a century of military and political upheaval known as the mid-third century crisis. Alexander Severus was succeeded by Maximinus, a brutal, wild, uncultivated and uneducated officer who rose from the ranks to become the first of a long line of soldier emperors[1].

A revolt against Maximinus in Thysedrus (al-Jem) in Tunisia led to the proclamation of the proconsul Gordian and his son as co-emperors. Gordian I and Gordian II reigned briefly and were followed by two emperors chosen by the senate. Two successive uprisings led to their assassination and the proclamation of Gordian I's grandson (or possibly grandnephew) as Gordian III.

Gordian III went to war against Persia and was killed in battle, whereupon Philip the Arab, Praetorian prefect, was raised by the soldiers to the purple.

When Philip came to the throne the empire, in the words of the third century sophist Nicagoras, 'was tossing as in a great storm or earthquake and floundering like a ship being carried off to the end of the earth'. Philip rode the storm for five years. Again, in the words of Nicagoras, 'Philip, as the most experienced of emperors, and one of superior intelligence... checked and stopped the rush in that direction, he brought her back and secured her at anchor.'[2]

It was Philip's fortune to celebrate the millennium of the foundation of Rome in AD 248, and to preside in unsurpassed magnificence and splendour over the ceremonies, secular and religious, of the eternal city, the last ever such celebration of the glory of Rome.

But Philip was an Arab, and this fact has provoked, with some notable exceptions, an avalanche of prejudice, calumny and abuse from both ancient and modern Western writers. He was also born a Christian, amid a large Christian Arab community in the Hauran, eighty years before Christianity became the official religion of the Roman Empire. Although his Christianity was private and unofficial, it aroused great enmity.

There is no existing biography of Philip the Arab, and his reign has been obscurely recorded and largely dismissed. It has not been easy, therefore, to resurrect the image of the man and his times from sources which are ambivalent, dubious, scanty, prejudiced and often abusive. In this portrait of Philip and his lost age, the themes which directly or indirectly influenced his life are dealt with briefly. If his Arab background has been stressed, it is because there is a discrepancy between the important role the Arabs played in eastern Roman history and the denial of this by most scholars; Philip's Arab background is used to provide a perspective for a greater understanding of his acts and his time.

It was not by magic that Philip sprang from an insignificant corner of the Roman Empire to rise to the highest position in the world. Behind him lay an extensive Arab presence in the Fertile Crescent. There were Arab tribes scattered over Syria and Iraq besides the three 'Arabias' outside the Arabian peninsula: the Arabian province in south Syria, which replaced the Nabataean kingdom; the Beit Arabiya in Iraq, which loosely included Edessa, Singara and Hatra; and, in Egypt, the nome of Arabia, lying between the Nile and the Red Sea.[3]

The literal sense of Hellenism, the merging of Greek civilization with the Near East, was mainly achieved in Syria through the Arabs, although the Aramaeans are often given the credit. Greek mythology, architecture and art entered Syria, and the natives incorporated classical Greek themes into their existing beliefs. Meleagare, the poet from Gadara (Umm Qais) in Jordan wrote, 'The island of Tyre is my nurse, but the country that brought me is Attica, installed by the Syrians in Gadara.' This process of assimilation and adaptation is most evident in the art and architecture of the period. For example, a lintel in Soueida in the Hauran shows Dusares, wearing a Phrygian cap, between the two daughters of Belshamin, Allat (Athena) and Astarte (Aphrodite). If some Western authors here considered themselves the only guardians of and heirs to the Graeco-Roman tradition, relegating the Semitic Arabs to an insignificant role, it befits them to remember that the Arabs enjoyed a thousand years of Graeco-Roman hegemony in Syria between the third century BC and the seventh century AD, and justly considered themselves heirs to this tradition; the Western association with the tradition began centuries later during Roman domination.

Oriental Arabs, urban and nomadic, cannot be considered barbarians, as they were heirs and survivors of ancient civilisations long before Hellenism and before the conquest of Rome.[4]

The Romans, in their conquest of Arab territory, took on the role of protectors of Hellenism and, intolerant of other powers in the area, gradually crushed Hellenized Arab kingdoms and principalities: Nabataea, Iturea, Osroeni, Emesa and, the last to fall, Palmyra. The Roman conquest of Nabataea and Palmyra delayed for seven centuries an Arab revival; only with the coming of Islam did the Arabs regain their natural hegemony over the fertile crescent.[5]

That Philip emerged from a thoroughly Hellenized class which the Romans found after their conquest of the Hauran, his birthplace, is clear, and that he became a Roman soldier, fighting to safeguard the empire, seems a natural development.

The spread of Christianity among Arab tribes in the first, second and third centuries in the Hauran was phenomenal, but is rarely acknowledged. It is also no surprise, therefore, that Philip should have been born a Christian.

In researching Philip and his time, one encounters radical contradictions in the sources. The same event is recounted in various ways, worlds apart. As to primary sources, besides the coins, inscriptions, portraits and monuments, the two primary literary sources are non-Western. Persian inscriptions and reliefs, and the XIII Sibylline oracle, written by Greek-speaking native Syrians. Both date from the third century, a few years after Philip's death.

The Greek and Latin sources were written in the fourth century, one hundred years after his death, and appear to have been based largely on rumour and legend. These classical sources were followed by Byzantine authors in the fifth, sixth and twelfth centuries, and by modern Western historians from the eighteenth century to the present, though all these must be considered secondary sources.

I believe that the true story of Philip's life has been completely distorted. The official story of the time denied the crushing defeat of the Roman army by the Persians and the death of the young Emperor Gordian III in battle (trampled under the hooves of Sassanid horses), and instead blamed his death on Philip who supposedly incited Roman soldiers to kill him, so as to take his place. The defeat was ignored, and the myth of Philip's perfidy created. If Philip was subjected to prejudice by Western authors, he was ignored and neglected by Arab historians, in line with their general indifference towards pre-Islamic Arab history, vast areas of which remain unexplored. Chairs of pre-Islamic Arab history do not exist at most Arab universities.

Many images of Philip emerge from the sparse facts recorded, but the most haunting is of a moderate, humane and just man, alone in his struggle against the odds – a crumbling empire, a ruined economy, sedition, usurpation, betrayal, prejudice and denigration – and standing fast against the tide.

CHAPTER ONE

DENIGRATION AND PREJUDICE

'He hails from Arabia, a wicked country.'
Zosimus, *New History*, 18.3

It seems only fitting to begin this study with an account of the denigration and prejudice to which Philip was subjected. We have no record of the Roman reaction at the time of his elevation to the purple, but they probably reacted as they had to other alien emperors who had reigned before him – the four African/Syrian emperors, Marcian the African and the barbarian from Thrace. But a hundred years after Philip's death, gossip was circulating all over the empire blackening his memory. Erroneous rumours were officially started by Decius and then fanned by Roman xenophones and fanatic pagans, for in their eyes Philip had the double misfortune to be both an Arab and a Christian.

Historians, with some notable exceptions, were bitter and resentful that the son of an Arab tribal chief from an obscure corner of the empire, the Hauran or the Leja (ancient Trachonitis), had acceded to the purple, that he negotiated with the Persians a Roman peace and, above all, that he presided with the Empress Otacilia and his young son and co-emperor Philip over the celebration of the thousandth anniversary of the birth of Rome.

From Cicero to the Byzantine Zosimus[1] and from Edward Gibbon to the present, Arabs have been generally regarded as plunderers. The epithet 'Arab' is joined to Philip's name in a perjorative sense. The word was a term of abuse, had unpleasant connotations to a civilized man, and was a common name for slaves.[2]

In the Sibylline oracle, Philip is called 'Syrian' instead of 'Arabian', disregarding the Roman administrative units: Coele Syria, Syria Phoenicia, Arabia, Palestine and the Lebanon. During the reign of Antonius Pius, Ptolemy, the geographer, placed the Decapolis and the Hauran in the province of Syria instead of in Arabia, which shows how eager people were not to be associated with Arabia and thus be called Arabs. The inhabitants of the more civilized parts of the province of Arabia referred to themselves as Syrians, an attitude reflected in the Sibylline oracle's description of Philip.[3]

The first primary source on Philip was written a century after his death by the fourth century writer, Eptomater, who is believed to be Aurelius Victor, the author of Caesaribus. He describes Philip's origin as 'exceedingly humble' and calls his father, Julius Marinus, 'the chieftain of a company of brigands'.[4] We can date these remarks because the author writes, 'In my lifetime the eleventh anniversary of Rome passed like an ordinary year, and was not marked by any official ceremony.'[5]

Also in the fourth century, the Augustan History[6] describes Philip as 'low born'. The same history, in the biography of Aurelian, lists Philip under the bad emperors, and says of father and son, 'who can endure the Philippii?'[7]

Two Latin authors, also of the fourth century, Eutropius and Ammianus Marcellinus, were likewise hostile to Philip. Ammianus, a Greek-speaking native of Antioch was derogatory about the Arabs as a race, calling the desert tribes 'scaenti' and 'saraceni' and describing them as feeding off wild game and plants, practising strange social customs and sexual extravagances. They were seen as homeless vagabonds, hostile and disruptive to the civilized world, like birds of prey sweeping down on the Roman countryside.[8] Ruffus Festus, in his Brevarium, repeats the Latin view.[9]

Zosimus, a Byzantine writing in the late fifth century and a pagan two hundred years after Christianity became the state religion, was similarly hostile to Philip. 'Philip hails from Arabia, a wicked country.'[10] His aversion to Philip is so great that he suppressed in his New History Philip's celebration of the millennium of the birth of Rome,[11] possibly unable to tolerate the fact that an Arab emperor could have lorded it over such a sacred Roman ceremony. To Zosimus, the elevation of Philip to the purple represented the barbarization of the empire at the highest level, and he describes Philip as a coward and spendthrift who made the throne a sort of family tyranny.[12] It is a dark picture indeed that he draws of Philip and of the Arabs.

Two Christian authors to write favourably about Philip, Eusebius and Orisius,[13] do not mention his Arab origins, presumably because they did not think highly of such origins. Eusebius speaks of the 'robbers of Arabia' and the 'barbarian Saracens'. The Christian Cronicon Pashale calls the Saracens barbarians; it reports that Decius transported lions from Africa to the eastern frontiers and unleashed them against the Saracens, the barbarians that dwelt from Arabia to Palestine, to Cirecium on the Euphrates.[14] St Jerome, who also wrote in the fourth century, takes a dim view of Philip and the Arabs. He states that Philip was the first Christian Roman emperor, but that in his early life he was a robber by profession.[15]

Modern Western writers have far outdone classical authors in their denigration of Philip and the Arabs. In the eighteenth century Edward Gibbons echoes St Jerome, stating in his *Decline and Fall* that 'Philip was an Arab by birth, and consequently in the earlier part of his life, a robber by profession.' Prejudice against the Arabs in general occurs throughout his work, with comments like 'from Mecca to the Euphrates, the Arabian tribes were confounded by the Greeks and Latins under the general appellation of Saracens, a name which every Christian mouth has been taught to abhor.' [16]

Twentieth century historian J. B. Bury, follows in the footsteps of Ammianus Marcellinus sixteen hundred years earlier: 'The great desert from Syria to the Euphrates was the haunt of Nabataean Arabs, known to the Romans as Saracens or Scaenites.' Quoting Ammianus, he describes their life as 'a continuous flight', and brands them 'barbarous undesirables, either as friends or foes', who played the same part in the Near Eastern wars as the Red Indians tribes played in the struggle of the French and English in North America.[17] It is difficult to accuse such an eminent historian of partial ignorance of pre-Islamic Arab history; such statements can only be attributed to prejudice. Jacob Burckhardt, quoted by Lissner, wrote: 'It is doing him [Philip] too great an honour to regard him as an Arab Sheikh; he came from a disreputable tribe of Southern Jordan.' Lissner himself adds that 'Philip was uncouth, ill-bred, arrogant and ruthless.'[18] Aube continues the litany: 'Philip is the son of a chief of brigands, a bedouin tribe of nomads and pillagers'. He describes Philip as 'perfidious, ambitious and without scruples'.[19]

The list continues with de Blois, who states that '[Philip's] dynasty had no traditional authority, originated from an obscure part of the empire which may be regarded with suspicion.' He follows Zosimus in his description of Philip as 'a coward and a spendthrift who made the emperorship a sort of family tyranny.'[20] Pohlsander writes, 'An aversion to bloodshed does not seem to have been a part of his [Philip's] character.' [21]

Philip's physical appearance is not spared. MacDormet describes Philip, kneeling before Shapur, as having 'a short cropped beard, and generally uncouth appearance, grossier, frustre'.[22] Of his portrait, Grant sees a 'new and non-Roman character with a highly charged expression, eloquent of suspicion and repressed turbulence flickering on his mobile features'. Grant goes on to say of a crisis which faced Philip: 'these emergencies were more than his mental and physical condition could bear'.[23]

Some modern historians seem more incensed than classical authors by the celebrations of the millennium under Philip's rule. With the exception of Zosimus, the ancients accepted Philip's celebration of the millennium as natural and in the order of things for a Roman emperor. Not so the moderns; Olmstead, for one, wrote, 'Irony enough when the coins bore the busts of Philip's ex-bandit father, the god Marinus, carried to heaven by the imperial eagle, crowning irony of ironies, when the Arab himself on 21 April 248 celebrated the thousandth anniversary of the imperial city's foundation by those secular games which Augustus had inaugurated for the preservation of the Italian character.' [24] Colin Wells says, 'In 248, by the irony of fate, it fell to the Bedouin Sheikh to preside over the celebration of Rome's thousandth anniversary.'[25]

The indignation is carried still further in the *Cambridge Ancient History*: 'Two hundred and fifty years since Augustus celebrated the birth of a new seculum, a century from Antoninus Pius, he who bore the name of Augustus was an Arab and, however closely he may have identified himself with the duties of his imperial situation, yet the true Rome and the Roman character to which men thought in these days they were doing homage, remained for him and must remain foreign.' [26] The Danubian troops, we are told, had a 'distaste for this Roman from an oriental province'. Curious, then, that these same troops did not show such racist antipathy when they elevated Philip to the purple in Persia!

Philip, Emperor of Rome, has been seen by some as the revenge of the Near East on the West and this is best expressed by Couple and Frezoulis writing about the theatre of Philippopolis: 'The spirit of the theatre never responded in the Orient to a need of the local population, but it imposed Western taste in the first two centuries of the empire. The Orient took revenge and imposed its men and women on the Occident, expansion of Oriental religions, an Oriental emperor!' [27]

CHAPTER TWO

ARABS BEYOND ARABIA

CONTRARY TO what some historians have implied, the rise of the son of a bedouin sheikh from the fringes of the desert beyond the Arabian peninsula was not such an isolated phenomenon, nor was Philip from a marginal people. He originated among the Arab groups who ruled a great part of Syria and some parts of Iraq and Egypt before, during and after his reign.

The Arab presence in the Fertile Crescent has been poorly and confusingly described by historians.[1] Arab tribes were no newcomers to the region; they had been there before and during the Neo-Babylonian period of the seventh century BC. The Assyrian king, Assurbanipal, razed the Sabaean colonies north of the peninsula – Yabroud, Amman, Moab and Edom – because the Arab tribes had collaborated with the Babylonians against the Assyrians, and, when defeated, had taken refuge with the Nabataeans. The Nabataean chief, Nadu, declared himself a vassal of Assurbanipal, but this was merely a pretence; the Nabataeans, together with other tribes, immediately rose against Assyria. The Assyrians were swift to act: they entered Arabia and, at the battle of Najd, the Arabs were defeated.[2]

Arab tribes were present in Syria during the Persian period. An Arab mercenary in the Persian army wounded Alexander the Great during the siege of Gaza. The notion that Arab tribes poured into the

Fertile Crescent with Islam in the seventh century is only partly true, for some Arab tribes were already established there. Their presence was ignored or obscured by classical authors who represented the Near East as peopled only by Aramaeans (or Syrians) and, later, Greeks.

The Aramaeans, the indigenous people of central and north Syria, were certainly the most important element within the population of the northern Levant in the first millennium BC. Their city states, such as Damascus, Aleppo and Hamath, were immensely powerful, and at the height of their power, they dominated the entire region. Aramaic became the lingua franca of much of the Near East. The Arabs, in common with other settled and established groups, adopted the Aramaic language and absorbed many cultural elements from the Aramaeans. With the demise of the Aramaean kingdoms by the middle of the first millennium BC, however, other peoples took on a more significant role, and by the Roman period the Arabs can be seen as a major dynamic force. Their importance has been largely overlooked, most probably due to the persistence of Aramaean culture and the Aramaic language.

The Arabs were fragmented, and although they shared the same ethnic background, were variously known as Arabs, Ismaelites, Saracens, Scaenites (tent dwellers) and Taiyâyé (from the tribe of Tây). They were also known by the names of their tribes, kingdoms and principalities: Nabataeans, Ituraeans, Edomites, Palmyrenes, Osroeini, Emesans, Hatrans and Safaites. The assumption of Graeco-Roman names during the Hellenization of the area also helped to obscure their Arab identity. These Arab groups controlled between them a large part of the area from the Euphrates to the Nile, and would have been the natural successors to the Seleucid and Ptolemaic kingdoms, had there been no Roman conquest.[3] But they had to wait seven centuries for the rise of Islam and the realisation of their aspirations.[4]

SYRIA

Rulers

There were a great many tribal chiefs in Syria, but the following brief list of the most important rulers in north Syria who carved out territories for themselves between the Seleucid period and the Roman conquest gives an idea of the extent of the Arab presence in Syria. They were the first to resist Pompey around Mount Ammianus when he set out to conquer Syria.[5]

Aziz: ruler of an Arab group in the region of Antioch, south of the Taurus range, who played a role under the last two Seleucids;[6] *Zabdiel*: the Arab dynast who killed Alexander Balas; *Malchus*;[7] *Strato*: tyrant of Borea (Aleppo); *Alchaedamus of the Rhambaei:* in power at the time of the Roman conquest; and *Gambarus and Themella*: Arab sheikhs who built little kingdoms for themselves.[8]

Emesans

Suhaim, an Arab sheikh, carved out a principality at the break up of the Seleucid empire and reigned at the time of the Roman conquest. Pompey confirmed Samsigeramus in this principality of Emesa and Arthusa. His son, Iamblichus, held it in Julius Caesar's day. The last ruler abdicated under Vespasian and was not replaced.[9] The dynasty became well known when one of its members, Julia Domna, daughter of the high priest, became empress on marrying Septimius Severus. Her two sons, Caracalla and Geta, and two nephews, Elagabalus and Alexander Severus, reigned as emperors.

Palmyrenes

The Palmyrenes were a federation of Arab tribes established in the natural oasis of Palmyra, of which twenty-five are known,[10] and provide an example of the sedentarization of Arab tribes in the deserts of Syria[11] in the first century BC. Because of the exceptional nature and position of Palmyra, they controlled the desert to the south of Damascus with their mounted troops between Emesa and the Euphrates. A camel aristocracy, they had permanent markets in Babylon, Ctesiphon and the Persian Gulf. They established the shortest route between India and the Mediterranean and knew the road to Central Asia. At the Roman conquest, they provided their knowledge and the infrastructure necessary to enable the Romans to trade beyond the empire.[12]

Septimius Severus raised Palmyra to the rank of colony as 'Ius Italicum'. The city flourished in the second and third centuries AD and received immense revenues from customs and goods in transit. The Palmyrenes were highly Hellenized and adopted Aramaic for commercial reasons, making it an official language along with Greek. They possessed a Greek constitution and many took Greek names, but they preserved their Arab tribal organization. [13]

No Arab group before the rise of Islam reached the Palmyrene level of military efficiency and power[14] but Rome crushed Palmyra's expansionist dreams in the third century, and in the process destroyed a flourishing north Arabian civilization.

Edomites

The Edomites (later Idumaeans), one of the oldest Arab groups in Palestine, occupied Djebel esh-Sharâ before the Nabataeans. Diodorus speaks of the Dead Sea as being in the presumably Seleucid satrapy of

Idumaea. The two famous Edomite towns of Marisa and Adora rose to importance in the Persian period and owed their prominence to the south Arabian trade via Petra. By the end of the third century BC they were great centres of trade. The Sidonians had a flourishing colony at Marisa, as attested by the rich painting of their necropolis. John Hyrcanus, the Maccabee, captured Adora and Marisa and forcibly Judaized the Idumaeans.[15] In Pompey's settlement, the city of Marisa was restored, for he took back almost all the cities the Maccabees had conquered,[16] but he left the Idumaeans Judaized and they gradually lost their Arab identity, except for those who emigrated. Idumaean fame came with Herod the Great, whose father was an Idumaean and whose mother a Nabataean, who, with his dynasty, played an important role in the Hauran, in particular in the Hellenization of the Arab tribes.

Nabataeans

Philip was born in the Hauran, which was, for the major part of its early history, part of the Nabataean kingdom. The Nabataeans were one of the oldest Arab groups in the area. Their presence has been established in Trans Jordan and Sinai in the third century BC and it is not known how long they had been there at that time. They are mentioned in the Cylinder of Assubanipal as an Arab confederacy.

Some equate the Nabataeans with Ismail's son Nabaitho, from the Old Testament, but there is no historical basis for this identification.[17] They seem to have been largely nomadic and hostile to the sedentarized Aramaeans, but they had settled by the end of the third century BC and can be traced in the Hauran.[18] They ruled Damascus between 84 and 72 BC, only to be thrown out by Pompey.[19] The Nabataeans became a significant force in the second century BC, and the first known king was Aretas II. At the beginning of the first century BC they helped the Gazans against the Maccabaean Alexander Jannaeus.

They spoke Nabataean and, for their commerce, Aramaic. The Nabataean dialect began, however, to diverge from Aramaic and by the first century BC it had its own characteristics and its own distinctive script. There are differing opinions as to the relationship between Nabataean and Arabic. It may be seen as a return to the original language, a sort of progressive replacement, until all the Aramaic elements were substituted with Arabic.

The Arabic alphabet came directly from Nabataean. The earliest Arabic script, the inscription of Namara (AD 328) east of the Hauran, is written in the Nabataean alphabet.[20] The demise of Aramaic came after the fall of Palmyra in AD 272/273. For the desert tribes the hegemony was now in Hîra and the kings of Hîra made Arabic the official language. The Nabataean language was partly maintained until the fourth century AD, as inscriptions in Hegra, Bosra and Umm el-Jemal show.

Nabataean art, architecture, religion and trade are beyond the scope of this study. Architectural examples in the Hauran, however, include temples and sanctuaries, most notably the temple of Dushara (AD 29-30) at Si'a, and another sanctuary there which dominates the necropolis with a dedication to Belshamin.[21]

Following their conquest, the Romans allowed the Nabataean kingdom to exist as a client state: it lost only part of its territory, the 'Aurantides' in the Hauran, which was attached to the Province of Syria. It remained a client state for a century and a half. Its kings sent auxiliaries from time to time to assist the Roman armies operating in the neighbourhood.[22] Petra, their capital, was enlarged after the Roman conquest.[23] The end of the client state came when

Trajan ordered Palma, the governor of Syria, to subjugate Petra in AD 106, with the III legion Gallica: the legion IV Ferrata was stationed in the new Arabian province, which replaced the Nabataean kingdom.[24] Petra remained the capital in the newly established province, but the centre of gravity soon changed. The trade that had previously passed through Petra to Gaza was now going instead to the Egyptian coast by way of Bosra, which had been the second Nabataean capital before it replaced Petra as the capital of the Arabian province.[25]

With annexation, many Nabataeans emigrated to Egypt, Sinai and Hadjaz; others retreated further south into the Arabian peninsula. A Sabaean inscription indeed records confrontation with Nabataeans near Najran in Yemen.[26]

The Romans inherited the Nabataean desert patrol which they strengthened with more Nabataean personnel. Trajan had installed the legion III Cyrenia in the region and raised troops from the Nabataean army and supplemented it with auxiliaries. The Nabataeans were invaluable for their expertise in mounted archery and camel riding. The 'Ulpiae Petraerum' were Trajanic units from Petra and were used elsewhere in the East to reinforce the defences.[27] Rome, as an internal police force, built the fortifications that align the Via Nova Traiana. Between Aila and Basra, Castella, forts, towers, mansiones (government inns) demonstrate the need to protect travellers from the attack of bandits.[28]

The crushing of the Nabataean kingdom had arrested the possible development of a civilized state of Northern Arabs.[29] Philip was born in the Arabian province which replaced the Nabataean kingdom in AD 204, almost a hundred years after its annexation; it was a period in which Bosra flourished and Petra was enlarged. A sad testament to the crushing of the Nabataeans by the Romans is the derogatory term

'Nabt' in late Arabic literature which designates 'villagers and hired workers'. The term may well reflect the fate of the remnants of the Nabataeans after the annexation and the departure of the aristocracy.[30]

Ituraeans

The Ituraeans were tribes of Arabs who inhabited the Lebanon and Anti-Lebanon and the hill country of the south, and the upper waters of the Jordan in northern Palestine. As nomads, they settled within the region of Aramaean culture and absorbed Aramaean elements. Thus, the proper names of Ituraean soldiers, as found in Latin inscriptions, are often Aramaean.[31] Both Strabon and Dio Cassius refer to the Ituraeans as Arabs.[32] They are called 'yzr' in Safaitic texts, the Arabic for Yatur (Aramaic),[33] and were unruly and given to brigandage. Alexander the Great was obliged to leave the siege of Tyre to conduct a punitive expedition against them.[34] They disappear from history until 115 BC, when their princes obtained recognition from the Seleucids. The princes were also priests and had both religious and secular authority. Their religious capital was Baalbek (Heliopolis to the Greeks) with its temple to the sun, and the secular capital was Gerrha (Ain-Jar), Greek Chalcis.

The founder 'Monicus the Arab', identified with Manaeus, was a Hellenized prince who gave his son and his capital Greek names, 'Ptolemy and Chalcis'.

Under him and his son, Ptolemy Mennaeus (85-40 BC), the Ituraeans made extensive conquests east of the Anti-Lebanon. They occupied a large area including the towns of Maglula and Iabruda (both villages near Damascus still retain the same names, Malula and Yabrud) and Abila. They even threatened Damascus, forcing the Damascenes to call on the Nabataeans to protect them. In the south-east, they took Batanaea, Trachonitis and Auranitis (the Hauran)[35] from the Nabataeans. With the conquest of Nabataean territory, they became closely associated with them.[36] Two inscriptions from Atil in the Hauran mention Itureans. Aristobulus I,[37] the Jewish king and son of John Hyrcanus the Maccabee, attacked the Ituraeans in 104-103 BC and captured part of their territory, Galilee, which shared a frontier with Judaea.[38] Aristobulus, however, was not content with conquest alone; he judaized the Ituraean Galileans by force, just as his father had forcibly judaized the Idumaeans in 126 BC.[39] Jesus the Galilean was born almost a century after the judaization of the Ituraeans of Galilee and one wonders if he might not have been of Ituraean Arab origin. The possibility cannot be dismissed, for was not Herod the Great, king of the Jews and builder of the Temple, himself a judaized Edomite Arab?

The Ituraeans fared well in Pompey's settlement, for Ptolemy probably bribed Pompey with a payment of 1,000 talents to restore to him Gaulanitis, which had been taken by Alexander Jannaeus. In return for this the city of Canatha in the Hauran was released from Ituraean control, and became part of the Decapolis[40] in 63 BC. For three centuries Canatha was the only city of the district, until Philip founded Philippopolis. When Pompey reorganized the coast of Syria, he left a little tetrarchy in north Lebanon under Ituraean control. Arca, the capital, was named Caesarea, and under Elagabalus, it received the status of colony and issued colonial coins with the legend 'Caesarea of Iturea'.[41] The city of Arca was the birthplace of the father of Alexander Severus.

The Flavians incorporated the Ituraean territory in the first century AD , but fragments of the Ituraean principality passed into the Herodian family.[42] With the amalgamation of Ituraean territory with the province of Syria, and from the end of the first century or even earlier, Ituraean Alae and Cohortes made their appearance in widely separated provinces of the Roman Empire, in Pannonia in AD 98 and 139 and between 110 and 150-167 they also appeared in Dacia, Mauretania, Libya, and in Rome.[43]

The Hellenization of the Ituraean princes early in the first century BC, as reflected in their names, was carried to the conquered territories, Batanaea, Auranitis and Trichonitis, the latter being the area in which Philip was born. This was followed by the highly Hellenized Herodians. It is not, therefore, surprising that the tribe of Philip was Hellenized from the first century BC, and later followed by romanization.

Safaites

The Safaites were an Arab tribe who arrived in Syria during the Persian period, around 500 BC. Initially a handful only, they traversed the desert from the Persian Gulf and inhabited Nabataean territory,[44] becoming subjects and allies of the Nabataeans. They were shepherds who roamed from the east of Damascus to Wadi Sirhan, with concentrations in the Hîra[45] or black desert, but they became primarily resident in the Hauran region of the Safa area - hence their name. The Safaites spoke and wrote an alphabet derived from South Arabia and developed during the Babylonian era.

Spoken in the third century AD and lingering until the fourth century AD, the Safaitic Arabic dialect is known from rock graffiti. Thirty thousand Safaitic inscriptions (mentioning the camel, horse, donkey and wild animals including the panther, wolf and lion) have been collected from an area extending through Jordan, Syria, Saudi Arabia and Iraq. Of these, 12,000 have been published and show at least 140 tribal designations.[46] It seems that every ancient Arab could scratch his name on a rock.[47]

These inscriptions show affinity with the subcategory of Thamudic texts (Tabuki) from the fifth century BC to the second century AD[48] and impart information on the social and cultural state of the Arabs. These are full of genealogies, sometimes including a dozen generations from the first century BC to the fourth century AD, and invocations of the divinity – a sort of prayer for Lat or Allat, the great goddess of the Safaites. They implore her mercy and pray for prosperity and for her to accompany travellers on their journeys. A figure carved on one of the rocks shows a naked goddess, wearing a necklace, bracelets and anklets. She holds a sash in both hands and an inscription to the side mentions three gods – Gad-Awidh (god of the tribe Aweideni), Rahim, Yamit – and the goddess Roda. The Nabataean god Dusares was adopted by the Safaites, and Baalshamin was borrowed from the sedentary population of the Hauran, as venerated in the sanctuary of Si'a.[49] Some tribes were bilingual and wrote graffiti in Greek and Safaitic, while other wrote Aramaic and Safaitic. The Safaitic texts were more numerous than the Greek, but that they wrote in Greek at all, and so early, is an indication of the early Hellenization of those tribes who were an integral part of the Hellenized, settled population in the Hauran and not merely nomads on the periphery of the provincial borders.[50]

Safaitic inscriptions in Greek name the chief of the tribe as Phylarch, serving as the commander (strategos) under the Nabataean kings. The tribal cult dominates in terms of defence and attack. Rome used the nomads to defend the limes (defence lines) against other Arab tribes and against the Persians, which explains the term strategos. A Greek inscription in Tarba mentions 'strategos' of the nomads: another in the village of Rama mentions the strategos of the tribe of 'Audenoi'[51] or the tribe 'Aoud', 40 km north of Bosra. The inscriptions prove the persistence of religious habits and indicate that the members of the tribe served as priests in the local temple. One inscription mentions a pilgrimage by the inhabitants of Safa to the sanctuary of Baalshamin at Si'a.[52] The family 'hl, ahl' in the Safaitic script included seven generations of Safaites. The eighth generation constituted a new Safaitic tribe, and a feast was arranged to mark the event. This practice continues through eight centuries of Safaitic history.[53]

The god Shai-al-quam (who does not drink wine) is often mentioned, depicted in military garb, as the divine protector of caravans.[54] The Safaites' loyalty and tribal allegiance to their fellow Arabs, the Nabataeans, is attested by several inscriptions. Three Nabataean kings are named Aretas ('hrth'), Rabbel ('rb l') and Obedas. Pompey is mentioned once, and thirty inscriptions mention Rome, ('rum', 'Irm', and 'hrm').[55] The tribes 'Awdh' or 'Aoud', 'Amrat' (members of the tribe serving as strategos under Nabataean kings) and 'Ubaishat' are often mentioned. The tribe of 'Salam' is of particular interest because of its location in the region of Soueida, near Shahba, the birth place of Philip.[56] Another sedentarized tribe, 'Sawar', is located in the north east of Jebel Druze and the the tribe of Dabonites is attested in an inscription at Samad at Leja: Trachonitis (the proper name Dabanos) is found in Philippopolis and Bosra. Graffiti continued to be inscribed for the first three centuries under Roman rule.

Sedentarization took place early on. Tribes such as the Auodhenians and other Safaites were completely settled in the first century AD, and were integrated into the defence of the empire. Some tribes, however, continued their seasonal migrations[57] and often only a fraction of the tribe was fully settled. Although the Arab tribes were flourishing political units in the first three centuries of the Roman era, relations with Rome were sometimes strained. Safaitic inscriptions tell of refugees and rebels against Rome ('nfr mn rm' and 'njy mn rm' – meaning 'fled from Romans'). The opposition to the empire came from major tribes – 'Aoud', 'Daif' and 'Ubaishat' – all associated with the Hauran. It was largely a case of internal strife and the resentment of subjects. The Roman forts and garrisons strung out through Arabia are monuments to a rebellious citizenry in its opposition to Roman imperial authority.[58]

The population of the Hauran was essentially Aramaean, but included a very important Arab element (Nabataeans, Ituraeans and Safaites). The Safaites occupied not only the desert places in Trachonitis, but formed the sedentary part of the population, particularly in Jebel Druze (Auranities). Greek inscriptions show that villages in this region were founded by the Safaitic tribe 'Awdh'[59] and that Jebel Druze was a centre for the summer sojourn of the nomads.[60]

It is worth noting that Arab groups in Syria and Mesopotamia – especially Ituraeans, Palmyrenes, Hatrans, Osroenis and Emesans – spoke Aramaic and various Arab dialects, and absorbed Aramaean elements. So too did the Nabataeans, although they were less Aramaeaized than the Palmyrenes. The Safaites spoke Arabic rather than Aramaic, as did the tribes of Tannuch and Thamud. But to which of these Arab groups in the Hauran did Philip belong?

The answer is clear. Both the Nabataeans and the Ituraeans were completely settled and had, by the third century AD, lost much of their tribal bedouin culture. The Ituraeans indeed had become largely assimilated with the Nabataeans. The Hellenized sedentary and semi-sedentary Safaitic tribes on the other hand preserved the ancient tribal structures, political and social. If Philip had been a Nabataean Arab he would have been called 'Philip the

Nabataean'. The only known fact about Philip's family was that he was the son of a bedouin sheikh, a phylarch or strategos of the nomads, which fits well with the Safaitic structure and leads us to presume that Philip was from one of the major Safaitic tribes mentioned in the inscriptions. He would have spoken and written Safaitic, as well as Greek, Latin and Aramaic.

MESOPOTAMIA AND EGYPT

Edessa – Arab tribes penetrated Mesopotamia and Syria. Foremost among them was the Osroeni tribe which occupied Edessa, formerly a Macedonian city (130-132 BC). Their dynasty, the Abgarids, remained autonomous throughout the Roman conquest until AD 244, just prior to the accession of Philip to the throne. With the fall of the Abgarids, the Arab character of Edessa faded. Aramaic was the dominant language, but a dialect of Aramaic – Syriac – developed in Edessa and became the lingua franca of the Aramaean Christians in the Orient. [61]

Singara – capital of the Arab tribe, the 'Praetioi'.

Hatra (fortress of the sun) – an Arab city state which formed a sort of buffer state between the Persians and the Romans. Its priest kings called themselves 'kings of the Arabs'. It was a well-fortified city which became rich from trade and the pilgrimage to its temple of the Sun God. The people were Arabs who, like the Nabataeans, Palmyraeans and Osroeni, spoke Aramaic. More than 350 inscriptions from Hatra are documented, dating from the first to the third centuries AD, ending when the city was sacked and abandoned. Hatra had resisted two Roman emperors, Trajana and Septimius Severus, but fell to the Sassanids in AD 240-1, due (according to Arab sources) to treachery from within the walls. Its fall was one of the causes of the Persian war.⁶²

The nome of Arabia – a Ptolemic nome, occupied by Arabs between the Nile and the Red Sea, halfway between Pelesium and Memphis, with its capital Phacusa.⁶³

TANNUKH, THAMUD AND TÂY

Tannukh – a confederation of Arab tribes from North East Arabia, which migrated to Hîra in Iraq and thence to Syria to escape Sassanid rule after the conquest of Mesopotamia.⁶⁴ In spite of the security offered by Syria after the Roman conquest, the Tannukh maintained good relations with the ruling Lakhmid dynasty in Hîra and this remained their base.

Thamud – confederation of small social units in the north of Hedjaz, near the Nabataean territory.⁶⁵ The Thamud came from South Arabia, and belonged to the same group of tribes as the Lihyanites. After the collapse of the Nabataean kingdom they spread towards the Dead Sea. Theirs was an Arabic dialect called Thamudic and, like the Safaites, their inscriptions – about four thousand to date – are found scattered throughout the peninsula, mainly in the central and southern regions.⁶⁶

Tây – an Arab tribe which emigrated from Yemen to the north of Arabia and Syria. Syriac writers attribute their name to Arabs in general (Tâyayé).⁶⁷

CHAPTER THREE

Hellenization and Romanization

in the Hauran

A PERIPHERAL REGION of the Graeco-Roman rural world, the Hauran was divided into three regions: Batanaea, Auranitis and Trachonitis[1] (modern Leja) and is located in an arid and inaccessible volcanic basaltic plateau, south of Damascus. Trachonitis served as a refuge for brigands who were also shepherds in c.30-40 BC. These brigands hid in caves and pillaged villages and cities – including Damascus.[2]

Settlement of the Hauran dates from at least the fourth millennium BC.[3] Only much later was it overrun by Arabs, probably before the Persian conquest.[4]

The Ptolemies and Seleucids fought two hundred campaigns over south Syria between 323 and 363 BC. The region of the Hauran was in Nabataean territory under the Ptolemies who ruled southern Syria, Palestine and Phoenicia, while the Seleucids controlled northern Syria. Northern and southern Syria were united in 200 BC when Antiochus III defeated the Ptolemies at the battle of Panium.[5]

The rise of the Hauran in the Hellenistic period was due to its being part of the Nabataean kingdom and under its military control from the first century BC to the first century AD.[6] This was a period of colonisation; cities and semi-military towns were founded, and centres of agriculture emerged with a population of landowners. In the last century BC the Ituraean Arab princes captured the Hauran from the Nabataeans.

Under Rome, when Anthony became master of the Orient, he reorganised Syria and, in 36 BC, bestowed upon Cleopatra many regions, including the Ituraean kingdom of Chalcis, and Jericho, Jaffa and Gaza. But Cleopatra coveted the Ituraean territory of the Hauran. Ptolemy, the son of Monicus (or Mannaeus) the Arab had died in 40 BC and his principality had passed to Lysanias (a relative, or possibly his son) and in 35 BC Cleopatra persuaded Anthony to put Lysanias to death and grant her his territories. She did not administer the territory directly, but leased it to Zenodorus, probably a member of the Ituraean royal house, who inscribed his coins with the title 'Tetrach and High Priest'. Zenodorus was an unsatisfactory ruler and supplemented his revenues by taking a commission on the robberies of his subjects. The Damascenes, his main victims, complained to Augustus, who took the three regions, Batanaea, Trachonitis and Auranitis and handed them to Herod, the new king of the Jews, in 24 BC.[7]

One story relates how, after Cleopatra's death, Zenodorus sold the three districts for fifty talents to Obodas, a Nabataean Arab, so that the Hauran became Nabataean again, though the Nabataeans failed to obtain official recognition of the sale from Rome.[8]

Herod pacified the districts with exemplary vigour, suppressing brigandry[9] and forcing the inhabitants to earn their bread by agriculture. To check future unrest, he created military colonies near Trachonitis, and transferred to them 3,000 of his countrymen, the Idumaeans, and the Jews, who had returned from Babylon.[10] Thus the Hauran became a buffer state between Syria and the Nabataean kingdom.[11] However, the natives of the three regions of the Hauran rebelled against the Jewish king, which was mentioned in Safaitic inscriptions of 12 BC as 'Yhd'

(Jews) who plundered and set fire to the shrine of Belshamin.[12] The rebellion was crushed by Herod, but some rebels escaped to Nabataean territory and made devastating incursions into Judaea. Herod complained to the governor of Syria who ruled for him, and launched a punitive expedition, killing some 2,500 Nabataeans. In an attempt to forestall future rebellions, he again sent Idumaeans to police Trachonitis, but they were wiped out by yet another rebellion. Herod then planted a second military colony of Babylonian Jews, who had migrated from the Parthian empire, in Batanaea, and exempted them from taxes.[13]

The Hauran passed from Herod to his son, Philip the Tetrach, in 4 BC, and intermittently to other members of the Herodian house between AD 31-41 and AD 44-54. Between these periods the Hauran was under the control of the Governor of Syria.[14] On the annexation of the Nabataean kingdom by Trajan, the Hauran was added to the province of Syria until AD 195, when Septimius Severus returned it to the province of Arabia.[15] Thus, nine years before Philip's birth, Shahba in Trachonitis was in the province of Arabia. Though some sources claim that Trachonitis remained in the province of Syria until Diocletian in AD 295 and that Severus ceded to the province of Arabia only the northern part of Auranitis and the southern part of Batanaea,[16] the XIII Sibylline oracle (AD 253) categorically states that Philippopolis (Shahba) and Bosra were at the time cities of the Arabian province.

The Romans undertook the construction of roads between Aila and Bosra and from Bosra to Philadelphia (Amman),[17] to ensure the rapid movement of the army in the mountainous basaltic region, and to guard against marauders. The roads were constructed by the Antonines and maintained by the Severans, and were extended by Philip in the third century AD.[18] The Romans also established water stations, towers and castella, fortified and garrisoned by Roman soldiers. A new life blossomed and the old centres of trade grew rich. Now well protected, the inhabitants turned to agriculture. Arabian tribes exchanged their tents for stone houses and pushed back the desert to extend their cultivation. They grew olive trees, vines and cereals and manufactured woollens. Temples, some with adjoining theatres, were built to the native gods. In the larger villages, aqueducts replaced the old wells.[19] The abundance of ruins in the Hauran today indicates that it was a rich and prosperous agricultural region.[20]

According to Rinfleisch and Wetzstein, writing at the end of the nineteenth century, the flourishing of agriculture in the Hauran was due to the influx of Sabaean tribes from southern Arabia who had established colonies in northern Arabia that were razed by Assurbanipal, and who had presumably integrated with later waves of migrant Arab tribes. The Sabaeans brought new techniques to the region, building canals, underground aqueducts, terracing, and houses made from long, narrow blocks of stone with flat roofs of stone slabs.

Pierre Gentille, however, disputes this theory of migration and suggests instead that agriculture was developed by the indigenous population.[21]

HELLENIZATION

Hellenization of the Orient preceded the Macedonian conquest of Syria. The zeal with which the Canaanite/Phoenician cities adopted the Greek language and the Greek way of life reflects, at least outwardly, their openness to foreign influence. The taste of the kings of Sidon for Greek art is well demonstrated by their limestone sarcophagi, and the third century BC necropolis of Marisa in Idumaea, with its wonderful naturalistic wall paintings, shows a similar desire to acquire the new style.[22] The practice of assuming a Greek name in addition to the indigenous name began as early as the third century BC in Phoenicia, and the two names were often similar; Abdshamash became Heliodorus, Abdastart became Aphrodisias. These names illustrate a religious syncretism. Semitic gods and goddesses – Shamash, Tanit and Astarte – were identified with their Greek equivalents – Helios, Artemis and Aphrodite. At the beginning of the second century BC Tyre celebrated penteteric games of her own in honour of Heracles who was identified with Malkart.[23] Hellenization received further impetus from the conquest of the Persian empire by Alexander.

In the Hauran, the Hellenized tribes, like other tribes removed from their homeland, retained their political and social structures because of their proximity to the peninsula.[24] The oldest Greek inscriptions of the region – in Trachonitis, the most dangerous district – date from the late first century. The existence of villages inhabited by Greek-speakers in an inaccessible and infertile region is partly explained by the policy of agricultural colonisation by Herodians, who encouraged Hellenization, especially among the notables, though the majority, Nabataean and Safaitic, were less Hellenized.[25] The temple in Si'a, erected at the same time as the temple in Jerusalem by Herod, also shows this direct Hellenistic influence.[26]

There are approximately two thousand Greek and Latin inscriptions from the Hauran (the former mainly from the second century AD 27) indicating village communities (Kôme or Koinôn).

However Sartre states that the early use of Greek in the Leja is well documented in inscriptions of consecration, due to the first century AD integration of the Hauran into the Herodian realm, and to its periodical incorporation into the province of Syria, ensuring close contact with Hellenism and Rome.[28]

Greek inscriptions discovered in the Hauran have been dated to the first and second centuries (Sur in AD 75 and 80, Jeddel in AD 106, Mseikh in AD 133-136, and in Jrein in AD 140).[29]

The rapid penetration of Hellenism is manifested by the use of Graeco-Roman names, especially in the urban areas where they were used as status symbols. Similarly, Greek was used in private inscriptions, epitaphs and religious consecrations. The epitaphs in the Hauran often repeated 'nobody is deathless' and 'take courage, no one is without death on earth',[30] but often contain blunders and barbarisms.[31] The use of Graeco-Roman names in Leja and in Bosra and Umm Jemal does not, however, necessarily imply Graeco-Roman immigration. The base was Semitic, but the names were largely Arab.[32] In Leja, Semitic and Graeco-Roman names are found in equal numbers, according to Sartre,[33] although he states elsewhere that Graeco-Roman names account for only 32 per cent of the total.[34]

In summary, the tribal organisation was Hellenized and legalised along Greek lines. The tribe became a *fule* (θυλη), the clan *koinon* (κοινον), the sheikh *stragegos* (στρατηγος), or *ethnatkes* (εθναρης), and the larger village (κοωμαι) became *metrkoma* (μητρκωμαι). Every village had land owned by the villagers, members of the modernised tribe.

ROMANIZATION

Pompey, the conqueror of Syria, saw himself as a missionary of Greek civilisation, a founder of cities and a promoter of Hellenism.[35] But to his surprise, he found the Arabs (especially the upper classes) already Hellenized, and by no means could they be considered barbarians.[36] As for his dream of founding cities, he discovered great cities already established and highly developed; Petra and Bosra in the south, Palmyra in the north, the greatest caravan city of the Roman period, and Emesa, the seat of the Sun God and Canatha (Qanawat), in the Hauran. But if Pompey and Rome came too late to Hellenize Syria, they brought order and security to Syria and the Hauran, which encouraged the nomadic Arabs of the peninsula to settle in the region.

In the first two centuries AD, Rome maintained the status quo, confirming the dynasts who served Rome well and appeared to be philhellenes.[37] Protectorates and vassal states were created which allowed the Arabs to retain their own political and social structures. In the second century AD these states were incorporated into the empire; initially the Nabataeans, Ituraeans, Edomites and Emesans, followed by the Osroeni and Palmyrenes in the third century. After annexation, with military strategy in mind, Rome began the construction of roads. At this time, Latin inscriptions first began to appear. An inscription at Azraq in Jordan mentions five detachments of legions who were probably building roads in the Hauran. Mismiyeh (ancient Phanea) was a garrison town during the second century for detachments of the legions III Galica and XVI Flavia.[38] Inscriptions, one dated AD 177-8 and written by a soldier in the XVI Flavia stationed in Shahba has been found,[39] and another in honour of Julia Domna, written during the reign of her son Caracalla (AD 211-216) have been found. These show the early contact of the villagers of the Hauran with soldiers stationed there.[40]

Some villages, like those near the camps of the Syrian legions in Bosra, were centres for the recruitment of soldiers by Rome, and the border garrisons seem to have been largely composed of Arab soldiers. By serving in the army, Arabs became citizens, and later civitas. The soldiers were recognisable by their gentilic affiliation – Palmyran,

Ituraean and Thamudian Arabs.[41]

Arab tribal chiefs in Rome's service, familiar with the geography and desert warfare techniques, formed patrols to prevent peninsula Arab tribes wandering into Roman territory. On their return, Arab soldiers became benefactors to their tribes, according to many inscriptions from AD 213-214, and formed a privileged élite. One inscription speaks of a veteran of the tribe of Mozadenoi. As soldiers, the Syrians and Arabian were considered second only to the Romans.[42]

Between the first and fourth centuries, following their policy of involving senior members of society in administrative duties (with the possibility of becoming noblemen), the Romans encouraged villagers to form municipal councils. Many villages, however, soon rose to the rank of city, a sign of increased prosperity.

As already noted, most inscriptions in the Hauran were in Greek, the civil power was Rome, and the gods of the temples bore Semitic names. Temples in the Hauran during the second and third centuries show a similar amalgamation of oriental and classical features. They had a hexagonal court with two altars – a small one for sacrifices and a large one for banquets – two basins for ablution and ritual purification, and two isolated columns or betyls.[43] The chief Nabataean god, Dushara, the Sun god and god of the mountains, fertility and joy, was identified with Dionysius, one of whose main symbols, the wine cup, can still be found adorning lintels in many Hauran villages. In Petra, the chief centre of the worship of Dionysius, a feast was held during the winter solstice in honour of him and his virgin mother.[44] Other Nabataean gods included Allat (the goddess of war), el Uzza, (Venus), and Aziz, Athi and Ruda Aumus. In Petra, Hegra, Wadi Rum, Bosra and Adraha, there were rectangular or round representations of the betyl.[45] Other gods were

CHAPTER THREE

worshipped also – Qôs, an Idumaean god, Bol-Bel, a Palmyran god with Babylonian connotations, Jarihubôl, Malakbel, Aglibel (also from Palmyra) and Belshamin, an Aramaean god.

The positive aspects of military occupation in a frontier region such as the Arabian province, namely the Pax Romana, the protection of citizens and the stimulus to commerce, were offset by the annona militaris – special taxes for maintaining the garrisons – the requisitions of supplies and services, and the frequent arrival of expeditionary military units which made additional demands on the local inhabitants, especially when it came to transport.

In the third century, the period of principal concern to this study, the campaigns of Shabur I had a profound effect on Syria, Arabia and Palestine, all of which saw the withdrawal of troops to serve during the emergency. Conscription into the legions and auxilia was primarily local; the representatives of cities and landowners were obliged to furnish the quota of recruits or the equivalent in additional taxes. In response to these oppressive military demands many provincials in the East fled from their lands and from mounting debts. This caused economic distress, brigandage and the desertion of tribal units.[46] In this context, the resentment of the easterners against Priscus, Philip's brother and governor of the eastern provinces, for the high taxes he imposed to pay the tribute to the Persians, was the main cause of the two revolts in Syria during Philip's reign.[45]

On close analysis, the Roman policy in Arabia was one of low-grade colonisation. One outcome of this policy was that representatives from the province of Syria entered the Senate late in the first century AD, their numbers increasing under the Severan dynasty. But the deliberate exclusion from political advancement[47] of representatives from the Arabian province, even from the major Hellenized centres of Bosra, Petra, Gerasa and Philadelphia, had one notable exception – the advancement of Philip to the imperial throne.

CHAPTER FOUR

WAR AND PREJUDICE

GORDIAN'S WAR

GORDIAN III was proclaimed emperor in AD 238, as a somewhat convoluted consequence of the coup d'état against Maximinus at Thysdrus (el-Jem) in north Africa which had proclaimed the 79-year-old pro-consul Gordian I, and his 45-year-old son Gordian II, emperors. It is not known whether Gordian III was the son of Gordian II, or that of his sister. The two emperors had been recognized by the Senate, but Gordian II was killed at Carthage by Cappellianis, the legate of Numidia. On hearing the news, his elderly father, the emperor Gordian I, committed suicide. The Senate had then designated a commission of 20 consuls and elected from among them two emperors, Pubienus, aged 74, ex-prefect of Rome and twice consul, and Balbinus, 60 years old and twice consul. However, an uprising in Rome had imposed as Caesar the 13-year-old Gordian III, and when the two emperors Pubienus and Balbinus were murdered by the Praetorian guards, Gordian III was proclaimed Augustus.

The Roman world was in a state of excitement; the handsome, noble boy-emperor Gordian III was preparing for war. There was dismay and pity for his youth. He had just married the beautiful Furia Sabina Tranquillina, (probably on 30 August 241, though some authors put it at August 242), the daughter of his tutor Timesitheus. Timesitheus had become his Praetorian prefect and was the real governor of the empire, but it was the young emperor who would lead the Roman army to victory. It was seen as high time to put the Persians in their place, albeit a little late, for Carrhae and Nisbis had already fallen to Ardashir before the death of the emperor Maximinus in 238.[1] Ardashir's son, Shapur, taking advantage of the disarray of the empire, then invaded Mesopotamia, and conquered the kingdom of Osroene, followed by Singara and even threatened Antioch.[2] Persian provocation had reached the limit, and Rome could not remain silent. A counter offensive was being prepared and, in AD 242, the emperor solemnly opened the twin gates of the temple of Janus, a sign that war was declared, and marched against the Persians.[3] It was the last time in Roman history that this ceremony was observed.

Timesitheus, who was responsible for the preparation, was a shrewd and able man. He had great ambition for his son-in-law, the emperor, and wanted him to follow in the footsteps of Alexander the Great in reaching the Indus and perhaps even China.[4] The feverish preparations for war were not confined to Rome, but were most evident in the eastern half of the empire, where people lived under the terror of Persian invasions, especially in Syria and Egypt. Expectations were high; victory was in the making and, sure of the outcome, Plotinus, the Neoplatonist philosopher from Assyut, left his studies in Alexandria to join the expedition in the hope that after the Roman triumph he would be able to study the philosophies of Persia and India.[5] Timesitheus, a learned man who appreciated philosophy, invited him to join the suite of the emperor.

At the time that Gordian III set out for war, the situation was grave. The Persians, having invaded and captured Carrhae and Nisbis between AD 235-

238, had continued their push into Roman territory in Mesopotamia with a raid on Dura (Europos) in April 239. It is possible that Gordian III had already paid a short visit to Syria to review the situation. A revolt in Africa, and the capture of Hatra by Shapur, son of Ardashir, in 241 added to the young emperor's troubles. The movement of the Roman army to the east was a complicated matter; the armed forces took various routes at different times.[6] Timesitheus, an expert commissary, saw to it that nowhere was there a sizable border city unable to accommodate an army and an emperor of the Roman people and which did not have supplies of cheap wine, grain, bacon, barley and straw for a year: smaller cities had supplies for 30 or 40 days, some for two months, at the very least 15 days.[7] Timesitheus had wide administrative experience, for he had served under Alexander Severus and under Maximinus as vice procurator of Asia.[8] As a man of great culture Timesitheus had been selected to tutor the 13-year-old Gordian III, before becoming his Praetorian prefect. An inscription describes him as 'Father of the emperor and protector of the Empire'. With his experience of the East, he had chosen a nucleus of oriental officers, Syro-Arabs who, because of their military and administrative experience, their knowledge of the area and of eastern languages and customs, held the posts of command.[9] For these reasons, too, he had probably chosen Julius Priscus as a colleague before the Persian war. Priscus had helped to raise his younger brother, Philip, to the elevated post of deputy Praetorian prefect. It is probable that Timesitheus had encountered the two brothers during his missions in the East, during the reign of Alexander Severus.

The influx of Arabs, and indeed the presence of two Arab officers from the Hauran in the Roman army's high command was almost certainly due to the recent policy of Septimius Severus in Arabia, and the introduction of Arabs into the court of Rome.[10] The Severi emperors who had followed Septimius Severus had shown favour to the province of Arabia, especially as both Elagabalus and Alexander Severus hailed from Emesa, a close neighbour of Shahba. The father of Alexander Severus was an Arab from Arca, the Ituraean principality on the Lebanese coast, and his mother, Mamaea, was the niece of Julia Domna.

As a learned man,[11] it is likely that Timesitheus gathered officers around him who were cultivated and well-educated men, forming a circle of trusted colleagues and friends, with whom he planned and conducted the Persian campaign.[12]

The army was assembled most probably in Sirmium or Viminacium. The emperor with his huge army of regulars and auxiliaries went by land and took with him much gold. His young bride, in a glow of expectation and unaware of the terrible fate that awaited her, accompanied her father and husband. The two Praetorian prefects, Furius Timesitheus and Julius Priscus, also accompanied them, accentuating the importance attached to this new offensive, leaving Valerius Valens to stand in for them as vice prefect.[13] The emperor was attended by the legion Parthica II, acting as Praetorian guard. This legion, created by Septimius Severus, had a special relationship with the imperial house: it had accompanied his son Caracalla on the Parthian campaign. The legion's reserves, however, remained at their duty station in the Alban hills outside Rome. In a dedicatory inscription, an augur for the happy return of the emperor and the empress Sabina Tranquillina, appears the title of P. Julianus, 'Commander of the reserves', providing evidence that the regular equestrian prefect of the legion had left with the emperor together with the bulk of the legion's manpower.[14]

The exact date of the departure of Gordian III with

the legion II Parthica is not known. Legions in the field joined the army: detachments from X Gema, XIII Gemina, and II Adjutrix. Gordian marched into Moesia, to add the Danube legions, VIII Aug, III Flavia and VII Claudia. His march had been delayed by engagements on the Danube where, according to the Augustan History, he had defeated the barbarian forces, repulsed the Carpi and the Goths, and crossed the Bosphorus, setting out on the military road which ran from Nicomedia to Tarsus and Antioch. His pace was leisurely and he stopped at many cities on his way. At Side he founded the Isophythian games, and coins of Aspendus and Smyrna also mark his passage.[15] Finally, he reached Antioch where he spent the winter.[16]

Gordian III did not reach the theatre of operations in northern Mesopotamia, between Carrhae and Nisbis, until AD 242. A series of skirmishes took place at Ras Aina (Ras al-'Ain), the source of the river Khabur. Here Shapur was unsuccessfully attempting to lay siege. The Romans won a resounding victory. Timesitheus recaptured Carrhae, Nisbis (Septimia Colona) and Singara (Aurelia Septimia) and expelled the Persians from Roman territory.[17] The Persians defeat rankled with Shapur, leading to his later, terrible, revenge. The emperor began reorganizing the liberated territories before joining the army for the invasion of Persia. He briefly re-established the kingdom of Osroene, annexed by the Romans in 241, and restored Abgar Phraetes IX to the throne. Edessa, the capital, became a Roman colony, and busts of the emperor and his consort on coins indicate that the colony was a military headquarters.[18]

The victory of Ras Aina greatly affected the Roman world for, following the upheavals in the wake of the murder of Alexander Severus, it restored pride and self-confidence, and as Romans always did in times of crisis or triumph, they harked back to the glorious past. To commemorate the young emperor's connection with this past, portraits of Roman heroes such as Trajan, who struggled against the eastern barbarians, appeared on coins, and to celebrate the event there were Capitoline games in Rome, and Olympic Alexandrian/Pythian games were held in Borea in AD 242.

In the euphoria of victory, the army prepared for the invasion of Persia and the advance to Ctesiphon. But at that very moment Timesitheus suddenly died – of dysentery, influenza or some other disease.[19] Timesitheus had made the Roman State his heir and his property was added to the city purse.[20]

It is on the death of Timesitheus that Philip the Arab enters the stage. There is no record of his past: the one thing certain is that he had had a military career, probably a tradition in the family since the Roman conquest (again, evidence of the successful integration of the Arab tribes into the military defensive system). His father, a strategos of the nomads, had probably encouraged military careers for his two sons. Philip had married in 234, bore a son in 237, and must have been serving in the western provinces before he joined Timesitheus' inner circle of high command.

When Timesitheus died, Philip replaced him as Praetorian prefect, an appointment made by the emperor, though his brother Priscus probably helped. Thus two brothers were now Praetorian prefects, a unique case in the Roman army.

CLASSICAL VERSION

With the elevation of Philip to the Praetorian prefecture, the jealousy, prejudice and distortion began. He was first accused of having poisoned Timesitheus to succeed him. Aurelius Victor, the primary source of the classical tradition, wrote, 'Timesitheus died according to some by the perfidy of Philip, to others by illness. As Timesitheus suffered from dysentery, the doctors prescribed medicine for his intestines. This was substituted by other ingredients which made him worse, and he succumbed.'[21] Victor, who was by no means kindly disposed towards Philip, at least offered as an option Timesitheus' death by illness. The Augustan History asserts that Timesitheus was murdered by doctors who colluded with Philip to replace his medicine with poison.[22] This version of events has been followed by some modern writers such as Olmstead, de Blois and Aube[23]; others, however, state he died of dysentery.[24] The accusation of poisoning is surely refuted by the actions of the emperor Gordian himself, who loved Timesitheus as a father and would not have replaced him by Philip if he had had any suspicion of foul play. The emperor must have known that Philip esteemed Timesitheus as a benefactor and loved him as a friend.

This first accusation of poisoning was but a prelude. The two brothers, as Praetorian prefects, were busy organizing and preparing the army for the invasion of Persia. The boy emperor had to master his grief over the loss of his protector and the father of his wife, and to lead the army towards Ctesiphon.

Following the Khabur river, they marched along the Euphrates, following the route taken by Trajan and Septimius Severus. The countryside they passed through was utterly desolate, the retreating Persians having adopted a scorched earth policy. It was, in any event, the wrong time of the year for an invasion in that part of the world. The climate was harsh and uncertain, and there was a lack of supplies as they crossed into enemy territory. Tired and hungry, disgruntled and dispirited, the army mutinied and the famous bread riots ensued, during which the classical authors assert that, at Philip's instigation, the emperor was murdered by soldiers. The facts were otherwise. It is likely that there were bread riots, but these were controlled before the army entered into action in enemy territory. At the battle of Misikhe, the two forces engaged and the Roman army was routed. The young emperor was killed in battle, and a large number of officers and men were taken prisoner. The soldiers, shamed and desperate, turned to the one man who, in their estimation, could save the situation, Philip the Praetorian prefect. They raised him to the throne with no opposition. At this point we see the chasm between fact and fabrication.

The historical Graeco-Roman tradition ignores the battle of Misikhe and the colossal defeat of the Roman army, concentrating instead on the murder of Gordian and the elevation of Philip to the throne. Here again we meet Aurelius Victor, who maintains that the Roman camp was ravaged by famine because of Philip's treachery, suggesting that Philip acted with Altho Marcellos, the commander of corn ships on the Euphrates, to ensure that supplies were not delivered. Hunger led to rebellion (instigated by Philip) and to the execution of the emperor. 'Philip, after creating an artificial shortage of supplies for which he blamed Gordian, had the emperor killed. . . he [Gordian] died victim to the intrigues of the Praetorian prefect.' The Latin point of view, hostile to Philip, followed Victor in the latter half of the fourth century. The *Augustan History* states that Philip could not contain himself in his sudden rise to office of Praetorian prefect, he began to plot through soldiers against Gordian, he intrigued to have the corn ships turned away and the troops moved to stations where they could not get provisions, and spread the talk that Gordian was young and could not manage the empire. The soldiers called him to the throne and Philip was entrusted with sovereignty, but the soldiers ordered that he and Gordian should rule together with equal rank. Philip began to bear himself arrogantly towards Gordian.

CHAPTER FOUR

Gordian knowing himself to be an emperor, an emperor's son and a scion of a most noble family complained bitterly to the soldiers and asked them to make their choice, but after Philip's intriguing he came off second in the vote. He then asked that their power might at least be equal, but he did not secure that either; he then asked to be given the position of Caesar but he did not gain this. His last prayer was that Philip should make him a general and let him live. To this Philip almost consented at last. Philip had him carried off then despoiled and slain.'[25]

Both authors ignored the battle of Misikhe and the Roman defeat, concentrating instead on the so-called treachery of Philip; they played on the contrast between Philip and Gordian, the noble boy, scion of the most noble family, versus, by implication, the upstart Arab!

Eutropius (late fourth century) in his *Brevarium* echoes the refrain: 'Gordian successfully humiliated the Persians in a momentous battle [Ras Aina], but as he was returning not far from the Roman frontier, he was killed through the treachery of Philip who ruled after him.'[26] Eutropius either ignored or was unaware of the Roman defeat, chosing instead to glorify Gordian's deeds. Ruffus Festus, also of the fourth century, wrote in his Brevarium, 'Gordian was assassinated due to the perfidy of Philip, his Praetorian prefect.[27]

The Greek author Ammianus Marcellenus who, together with Eutropius, joined the campaign of Julian the Apostate against Persia in AD 360, and visited Gordian's monument with him at Circeium, more than a century after the event, took his version of Gordian's death from the speech of Julian to his soldiers at Circeium — a speech in which he, a Roman emperor, ignored the Roman defeat at Misikhe and Gordian's death on the battlefield, so as not to dishearten his army on their way to fight

57

the Persians.[28] Ammianus wrote of Gordian, 'After vanquishing the Persian king, and putting him to flight at Ras-Aina. . . he was struck by an impious wound inflicted by the faction of Philip, the Praetorian prefect and a few wicked accomplices, in the very place where he now lies buried.'[29] Both writers saw Gordian as a hero and ignored the battle of Misikhe.

Paulus Orosius was an exception among fourth and fifth century authors. He did not accuse Philip of Gordian's death, but presented him as a Christian emperor.[30] But Zosimus in the fifth century repeated the fanciful story of the *Augustan History*: '. . . he ordered the ships of provisions to go on, so that the army, oppressed by hunger and want of supplies, might mutiny. His plan worked, the soldiers mobbed Gordian and killed him and they conferred the purple on Philip.'[31]

The Byzantine version of Gordian's death differs from the traditional Latin version, and is nearer to the Persian account of events.[32] It is best represented by the twelfth century Zonaras who reported in the *Annals* that 'Gordian was accidentally wounded in the campaign against the Persians, he was taken to Roman territory where he died of his wound.' Zonaras did not use Philip as a scapegoat and corrected the errors of ancient writers.[33] Zonaras also reported that the Senate named two successors to Gordian, both of whom died before Philip came to Rome.[34]

It is curious that in the classical sources there is no suggestion of the Roman defeat in the Persian campaign. The XIII Sibylline oracle does not mention this mishap, which shows that ignorance was widespread even among contemporaries.[35] The fact that Julian the Apostate would go out of his way to visit the monument built for Gordian, and that both Eutropius and Ammianus would recall Gordian as a hero of the wars with Persia, further suggests a long-standing distortion of historiography.

The Sibylline oracle, the only contemporary literary and primary source, written in AD 253, four years after Philip's death, attributes Gordian's death to unspecified treachery, but is definite that he fell in battle,[36] although there is no mention of a Roman defeat. The effect of imperial control over such information is admirably illustrated by this lapse.[37]

In summary, according to classical historical tradition, Philip is accused of having poisoned Timesitheus and taking his place as Praetorian prefect, and, further, of having instigated the murder of Gordian and taking his place as emperor. To do so, he cut supplies which caused a mutiny, as a result of which Gordian appointed him as his colleague, a fanciful description without parallel elsewhere, and none of it need be believed.[38]

In reality, Philip was elevated to the throne in very unfavourable circumstances, after the defeat of the Roman army, by soldiers in a state of disarray, despair and shame. The soldiers sorrowed for the 19-year-old emperor, trampled and killed under the hooves of Sassanian horses. They sympathised with Philip, who had been obliged to kneel in submission and plead with the Sassanians[39] and preferred Philip to his brother Priscus, the other Praetorian prefect, possibly because of his mildness and moderation.

Between 13 January and 14 March 244, Philip found himself emperor in enemy territory, with a mutinous and disorganised army and his fellow officers prisoners of the Persians. He had little choice but to seek peace with the Persians. His task was to regroup the army, instil discipline, buy the liberty of the Roman prisoners, preserve the gains achieved at Ras-Aina and make a lasting peace[40] – and then to lead the army back to Syria.

THE PERSIAN VERSION

In 1938 an inscription was found carved into the cliff face at Naqsh-is Rustam, four miles from Persepolis. The text, in Arasacid, Pahlavi Sassanian and Greek, was published the same year and greatly revised the history of the Persian War as presented in its fabricated form by the Graeco-Roman authors. Modern historians have named the inscription '*Res Gestae divi Sapuris*' because it was modelled by the new master of Iran on the '*Res Gestae divi Augusti*' and engraved on the walls of temples in different provinces to mark the achievements of the founder of the Roman Empire.

The relevant part of the text reads as follows: 'When we were established in the empire, Gordian Caesar from all the dominion of the Romans, a force of Goths, and German people collected, and into Assyria against the people of the Aryans and us he made an inroad, and into the mountains of Assyria in the Misikhe from opposite, a great war arose: And Gordian Caesar was killed and we annihilated the army of the Romans. And the Romans proclaimed Philippus as Caesar, and Philippus the Caesar came for supplication and offering for the life of his friends five hundred thousand denarii. He gave them to me, and for tribute to me it shall be, and on account of this we named Misikhe Peros Shapur [Anbar, 50 km west of Baghdad].'[42] On the same wall is a relief, identified by Grishman, showing Gordian prostrate under the hooves of Shapur's horse. He is beardless and youthful – being only 19 years old when he died – which corresponds well with his coin portrait. Philip is shown in the relief kneeling before Shapur in supplication. The image corresponds with his coins and the busts in the Vatican Museum showing cropped hair and a generally uncouth appearance.[43]

The Persian account of the war, both inscription

and relief, represents a primary contemporary source. It shows the complete defeat of the Roman army and demonstrates a contrary view to the long line of Greek and Roman historians.

On the death of the emperor in the battlefield, Philip surrendered and paid a heavy tribute – according to the Persian text, 500,000 denarii in gold. The intriguing question is how, when they record the fact of the ransom and its payment in gold, the classical authors can deny that the Roman army was defeated? [43]

The two primary sources from the third century – the Persian inscription and the Sibylline oracle – state that Gordian died in battle.[44] The Sibylline oracle is cited by advocates both of Philip's guilt and of his innocence. Although it is believed that the XIII Sibylline oracle had more than one author, Olmstead holds the unsupported view that the author was Christian, and speaks of the Christian Sibyl, who would have had less reason than most to slander Philip, protector of her fellow Christians.

Olmstead cites as proof of Philip's guilt the verse, 'he will fall in the ranks smitten by gleaming iron, because of jealousy, moreover betrayed by a companion.' [45] But Olmstead overlooks the fact that the same verse states that Gordian fell in battle – proof, surely, of Philip's innocence.

Apart from the Persian evidence to support Philip's innocence, it is hard to believe that a man who has killed his emperor would then build a monument to him at Circium, and carry his mortal remains all the way to Rome[46] for his memory to be revered rather than damned. Gordian did not suffer the damnatio memoriae. On the contrary, Philip requested the Senate to consecrate him among the Divi,[47] and similar respect for the emperor's memory was shown by Julius Priscus. Philip took care that no harm befell any of Gordian's entourage. Furthermore, his leisurely return to Rome is not the action of a man rushing to placate the Senate and conceal a crime.

That not everyone in the fourth century believed Philip to have been responsible for Gordian's death is clear from the eastern Roman emperor Licinius's claim that he was descended from Philip the Arab – a claim he would not have made had Philip been the monster and murderer portrayed by the classicists. Nor, indeed, would Philip have been enrolled with his son among the Gods, either by Licinius or Constantine.[48]

Traditions do not die easily, especially one seventeen hundred years old. The ignorance of modern historians writing prior to 1936 can possibly be excused, but those who persisted in their belief of Philip's guilt after the publication of the Persian inscriptions can only be called prejudiced. Rostovtzeff, for example, writing in 1957, states that 'Gordian was killed by soldiers in a bread riot, probably at the instigation of J.M. Philippus, a Praetorian prefect'.[49] Lissner (1958), says, 'Philip had the mortal remains of his 19-year-old victim taken back to Rome, informing the Senate that he died of disease.'[50] Brauer (1975) states, 'Philip persuaded the soldier to do away with the noble boy named Gordian.'[51] Furthermore, Sarre (1995), says that 'Philip was repulsed by killing Gordian, but it was the only solution.'[52] Oost (1958) in his enthusiasm to prove Philip a murderer, points to a passage of Porphyry's Life of Plotinus: 'When Gordian was killed in Mesopotamia, Plotinus escaped with difficulty and came safe to Antioch. After Philip had become emperor, he came to Rome at the age of 40.'[53] One wonders how such a passage in any way indicates Philip's guilt. Quite the reverse. If Plotinus went to Rome after Philip became emperor, it was precisely because Philip was emperor; both were Hellenized Orientals from Syria and Egypt, both had been in the circle of Gordian and Timesitheus. We know from Eis Basilia that Philip was interested in philosophy and it is very likely that Philip was a friend of Plotinus and welcomed him to Rome.

Oost, however, draws a fantastic conclusion from the passage, describing it as an original source by an eyewitness to Gordian's death and Philip's guilt. In reply, Potter says, 'If the phrase suggests that there was trouble in the camp after Gordian's death, and if Philip was involved with the trouble, it would be strange that Plotinus who had been incommoded by it should go to Rome, where Philip was at the time he arrived.'[54]

Perhaps the most extreme case of denial, however, is that of Pohlsander who in 1980 states, 'My own opinion is that Philip was guilty. Near-eastern royal inscriptions are notoriously boastful, Shapur's inscription is no exception, and thus suspect.' He then goes on to say, 'the inscription insinuates that Gordian died in battle, but stops short of saying that he was killed by Shapur.'[55] This last statement is amazing, to say the least. If Shapur did not kill Gordian in battle, is the author suggesting that Philip, the Praetorian prefect, killed his own emperor in the midst of the battle, in front of the enemy?

In addition to the authors quoted above, there are still more historians who accept Philip's guilt, among them Franz Altheim, Fergus Miller, H.M.D. Parker and B.H. Warrington.[56]

However, some reason prevails. Many modern historians, writing both before and after the discovery of the Persian inscription have exonerated Philip of guilt. Edward Gibbon (whose jibes did not totally spare Philip) was one of the earliest to see through the classical tradition. Two centuries before the Persian inscription was discovered he wrote, 'How could Philip condemn his predecessor and yet consecrate his memory? The *Augustan History* cannot in the instant be reconciled with itself or with probability. How could he order his public execution and yet in his letters to the senate, exculpate himself from the guilt of his death?'[57]

Potter, in his commentary on the Sibylline oracle, says, 'The fact that Philip honoured rather than damned, the memory of Philip, and that men who had been associated with the previous regime could continue to prosper, suggests that Philip did not have a direct role in bringing that reign to an end.'[58]

Many scholars have seen the Persian inscription as absolute proof of Philip's innocence. Maricq and Honigmen, in fully accepting Shapur's account, rationalize the Graeco-Roman tradition as having arisen to efface the memory of a military disgrace.[59] Sprengling sees no indication of treason on the part of Philip, nor of his having been at fault in the defeat, of any weakness on his part in concluding the peace and, least of all, of having had a hand in the death of Gordian, who is clearly represented as having fallen in battle. Again, he explains the version that Gordian was killed by Philip as a means of expunging a military disgrace.[60]

Swift points out that the research of Maricq indicates that the Sibylline oracle states that Gordian died in battle, and if Maricq is right, then Shapur's account must be true.[61]

De Blois accepts the Persian victory at the battle of Misikhe, where Gordian perished and Philip approached Shapur on his knees.[62] In the same vein, MacDermot writes that 'the relief of Shapur represents the emperor as dead beneath the feet of Shapur's horse.'[63]

York, one of the most ardent historians to vindicate Philip, says, 'The trilingual inscription and the illustrations in the reliefs of Naqsh-I-Rustam and Bishapur show that Gordian has been killed in battle in which the Persians were the victors.' York goes on to say that 'the official fourth century distortion of the dénouement of the Persian campaign of Gordian III was built on rumours which made Philip responsible for the death of Timesitheus, and tales of his putting a Persian

CHAPTER FOUR

hostage to death, or the slaying of the son of Gordian who was entrusted to him, and last but not least, the fictional version of the death of Gordian in a revolt of discontented soldiers, who killed the emperor and made the cunning Philip his successor, seemed both to cover up the defeat and to blacken the memory of Philip.'64

Others who accept Philip's innocence include Prickartz, Grant and Hermann Bongston.

Some historians were neutral on the subject. Bowersock writes, 'Whether Philip was privy to intrigues... that led to the death of young Gordian in the field is now beyond telling.'65 Shahid, an Arab historian, writes, 'Philip only connived at the murder of Gordian by the troops, who clamoured for a man to lead them, not a child.'66

To understand the acceptance of the Graeco-Roman version of events, one has to imagine the effect that a crushing defeat of the Roman army had on the crumbling Roman Empire. All hopes had concentrated on that army marching to defeat the Persians, headed by the noble youth, 'scion of Roman nobles' (as the Graeco-Roman writers called him) 'Beauty' (for he was a handsome boy, with a beautiful young bride), 'Wealth' (as he carried with him much gold). And with the boy-emperor had marched the pick of the mighty Roman legions, an army which Plotinus the philosopher had rushed to join. The army also carried the ambition of Timesitheus, who wanted his son-in-law to follow in the footsteps of Alexander in conquering Persia and reaching India. All these hopes had been crushed. Roman officers and soldiers had been taken captive by the Persians, chaos and confusion reigned, and in the aftermath of defeat Philip the Arab stood alone. By his determination and strength he had reassembled the shattered army, treated with the victorious Persians, arranged the ransom and organised the army's march back to Syria.

But this story could not simply be told. Seizing on

the fact that Philip was an Arab – an object of derision among literary circles of third and fourth centuries – he was vilified in order to put an artificial gloss on the military reputation of Gordian. The summary of events leading to Gordian's death were distorted to obscure his failure, and the emphasis placed on Philip's role in his death.

Decius, who betrayed Philip and instigated his murder in order to succeed him, continued to spread rumours of Philip's role in Gordian's death, thereby bolstering Gordian's reputation and mitigating his own betrayal and murder of Philip.

TREATY

On the subject of the treaty concluded by Philip with the Persians there is no agreement between historians. The key question is whether or not Roman territory was to be ceded to the Persians. There was certainly resentment to the treaty in the eastern provinces, and some called it shameful. According to Zosimus, Philip had not abandoned any territory to the Persians.[67] Many historians agree that it was not an embarrassing treaty, nor were its terms unfavourable to Rome, since it kept a nominal supervision over lesser Armenia and Mesopotamia. The treaty was clearly acceptable enough to Philip for him to feel justified in assuming the title 'Persicus Maximus'. His coins of that period bear the legend 'Peace with Persia'. In reality, he had no choice, but at least he appears to have concluded a peace on the best possible terms. Why Philip did not cede Nisbis or Singara to the Persians[68] is difficult to understand for, despite the Roman emperor's diplomacy and military manoeuvring, Shapur could not have planned to let him off so lightly, with a tribute of only 500,000 denarii per year and the stipulation that Rome keep out of Armenian affairs (a clause later tested when the activity of the governor of Cappadocia was seen by the Persians as unjustified aggression and interference in the Armenian affairs).[69] But the treaty must have demanded that the Romans abandon the area between Singara and the Euphrates and any Persian territory conquered by Gordian and not recovered by Shapur. Recent excavations of forts 30 km east of Singara at Ain Samu (in northern Iraq), confirm that Rome abandoned the region after the peace treaty of AD 244. At Tifrin, excavations of a fort constructed under Septimius Severus show that it was occupied until the reign of Gordian III; no Roman coins of any later date were found.[70]

This loss of territory aroused resentment in the Roman world. In the eastern provinces, which bore the brunt of the expense of the Persian war, resentment was particularly deep, especially after Philip had departed for Rome, leaving the East in the hands of his brother Priscus, as 'Rector Orientis'. Priscus's reign was known for its fiscal stringency, which added to the grievances of these provinces, already disturbed by earlier Persian incursions and the presence of the massive Roman army before and after the invasion.[71]

Zonaras confirms that Philip was forced to break the peace treaty in order to recover the lands,[72] and in the summer of AD 245, one year after the conclusion of the treaty, the lands ceded to Persia were recovered.

This recovery was probably made by Priscus, for there is no indication that Philip returned to the east from Rome. The date is of AD 245 is most likely since this is when Philip assumed the title 'Parthicus Maximus'.[73] Nisbis and Singara were given the title 'Julia'.

The immediate payment of 500,000 aurei (which figures in the Persian inscription as denarii) as ransom for the Roman prisoners, and the continuing subsidy, proved a great drain on the imperial treasury, particularly as the empire's resources had been greatly depleted by the campaigns in the East. Payment of gold ransom was nothing new to the Romans, for under Gordian III they had been paying a gold tribute to the Goths on the lower Danube – a tribute stopped by Philip in 248.[74]

The accusation that Philip concluded a hasty treaty so that he could return to Rome to placate the Senate is without foundation. His negotiations with the Persians were protracted and carefully calculated, and the theory is based on a misinterpretation of a dedicatory inscription 'Victoria Redux' found in Rome. The dedication is dated July 244 and has been taken by some as the date of Philip's return. But it is impossible that he could have arrived in Rome by that date, for he was only elevated to the throne by his soldiers between 13th January and 4th March 244, and subsequently had not only to negotiate the treaty, but also lead the huge army back to Syria.[75]

The inscription in question was dedicated to the new emperor and his wife by the veterans of the legion II Parthica, who had been left behind when the main force of the legion accompanied Gordian III to the Persian war. The veterans merely wished Philip a happy return to Rome. The first line reads, 'To the Victoria Redux of our lord imperator Caesar M. Julius Phillipus, Pius, Felix, Augustus and Otacilia Severa Augusta, wife of our lord.' The date of the inscription by no means implies that Philip himself was in Rome in July 244.[76]

In fact, Philip took his time in returning to Rome. In Syria, he visited many cities of his native Arabian province, conferred honours, initiated games, gave instructions for the construction of temples and roads, and ordered and planned the building of his new city Philippopolis. In a similarly leisurely manner he visited Antioch and the cities of Asia Minor. He received deputations and petitions, attended games, and did not reach Rome before the end of AD 244 or beginning of AD 245.

CHAPTER FIVE

ARABIA REVISITED

A FAMILY VISIT

HAVING CONCLUDED the peace treaty with the Persians in AD 244 and sworn friendship with Shapur, Philip set off for Rome. True to his prejudice, Zosimus says that Philip cultivated the soldiers with handsome gifts and sent messages to the Senate to say that Gordian had died of disease.[1] Before he left Persia, he made his seven-year-old son Caesar, then proceeded to Syria, the first stage of his homeward journey. Although there is no record of the last time Philip had been in his home country, the Hauran, it takes little imagination to presume that he was looking forward to returning home as emperor – and was anticipating with pleasure revisiting his clan and his village.

On his way home Philip ordered the closing of the mint in Edessa, which had been issuing coins in the name of Gordian III and Abgar X since 242.[2]

Philip's first stop was at Bosra, the capital of the province of Arabia, which he raised to the rank of metropolis (Petra, the old capital, was already a metropolis). There he established the 'Acta Dusaria', a festival in the Greek style for athletes and performing artists, designed to forge an ideological bond between Rome and Arabia, linking Augustus' victory at Actium with Dushara, the principal god of the Nabataeans.[3]

Philip was naturally eager to raise the political and

economic status of his countrymen and he is attributed with promoting, Odainatus II, a fellow Arab and chief of Palmyra to the Roman Senate. Odainatus became known as 'King of Kings' and the hero who defeated the Persians and saved Syria for the empire. In this case, as in many others, Philip the Arab followed in the footsteps of Septimius Severus, who had promoted the first Odainatus (father or uncle of Odainatus II) to the Roman Senate. In recognition of the honour bestowed on him, Odainatus adopted the name 'Septimius' and 'Septimia' for all the members of the ruling family of Palmyra.[4]

Philip also stopped at Damascus, which he raised to colonial rank[5], and ordered there an addition to the temple of Jupiter.[6] He also revived the 'Olympia Sebasmia' games, a festival celebrated in the reign of Elagabalus.[7] It is possible that Philip visited Neapolis (Nablus), a city in Palestine which he accorded colonial status, for the Olympia Sebasmia were also celebrated there.[8] Neapolis, Vespasian's new town, was built on the site of the village of Nabartha, close to the Samaritan Shechem.[9] The new city, according to the evidence of coins, was founded in AD 71/72, with a large territory stretching toward Scythopolis (Beisan). The population at that time seems to have been Samaritan, but a change occurred under Hadrian and his successor Antoninus Pius, for the coins show Mount Gerazim crowned by a pagan temple to Zeus Hypsislus, which suggests that Hadrian disenfranchised the Samaritan aristocracy which had ruled the city and entrusted its government instead to pagans – either the existing pagan population or new settlers. It is not surprising that Philip made Neapolis a colony, for it was an important city and is mentioned by Ammianus as one of the five main cities of Palestine.[10] The other four were also pagan cities; Caesaria, Ascalon, Gaza and Eleutheropolis (Beit Jibrin). From the evidence of coins, he may also have visited Ptolemias (Akka), on the coast of Palestine and probably visited Heliopolis (Baalbek), the ancient capital of the Ituraeans, for the circular temple in the sanctuary of Jupiter Helipolitanus is attributed to him.[11]

Finally, Philip reached his home and his family in Shahba. Once there, he ordered and planned the refoundation of his native village and gave it his name. It was to be the only totally new city erected in the mid-third century, a period of crisis, in contrast to the preceding hundred years during which many cities had been built over an extensive area.[12] The city was built less from necessity than to fulfil the fantasy of a soldier-become-emperor who wanted to confirm the lasting unity of the empire and to proclaim his pride in his origins. It was a gesture that ran against the tide, since Rome, in all other respects, was falling apart. Philippopolis was the creation of a would-be Roman,[13] who sought a place of honour for his family and his new dynasty. It was a city founded with a desire to promote the economy of the area, but above all to provide his fellow Arabs with the amenities of Roman civilisation.[14]

Philip's joy in visiting his family home was incomplete: there is no record of his mother who presumably had died – as had his father, Marinus. Philip's reverence for his father, and grief over his death were evidenced by the act of his deification (following the precedent of Trajan[15]), although Marinus had never reigned. Veneration for his father led Philip to build one of the most important monuments in Philippopolis, the Philippeion, which is identified as the tomb of Marinus. An inscription on the drum of a column is a dedication from the élite unit of the imperial cavalry, the Philippianae, to 'Divo Marino'. Another dedication by a person of consular rank, on the consoles of the mausoleum, twice repeats, 'Marinus the God'.[16] After Philip's successful campaign against the Carpi, the Senate acceded to Philip's wish, declaring his father divine[17] which proved to be of great advantage to the new dynasty Philip established.

Of Philip's clan, only his elder brother, Gaius Julius Priscus, is amply recorded. An inscription on a column in Palmyra and a dedicatory inscription in Rome name him 'Praetorian prefect, prefect of Mesopotamia, Juridicus in Alexandria, vice-prefect in Egypt, procurator of Macedonia and a legionary vexillation.' The distinguished posts he held, the highest in the empire, and the speed of his advancement, imply a man of considerable ability.[18] Both brothers must have served under Alexander Severus, an Oriental like themselves. The Severan interest in Syria is well known, and the brothers may have owed their military promotion to Alexander Severus. It is assumed that Philip remained in the army during the struggle for power between the two Maximini (AD 235-238) and of Pupienus and Balbinus (238), and the Gordians (238-244). To the Gordians, the brothers, by now both military officers, must have shown great loyalty, which surely explains their favour with Gordian III. Of their devotion to Gordian III there is no doubt, a devotion the boy emperor repaid by making them both Praetorian prefects.[19] It is an unanswered question why the soldiers chose Philip as emperor after the death of Gordian, instead of his brother Priscus, who was the more experienced and distinguished, for he had had a long and brilliant career. But Priscus's loyalty to his younger brother was exceptional and he appears to have shown no resentment at having been passed over.

One reason for the choice of Philip as emperor may have been his moderation and gentleness, in contrast to the severity of Priscus as a disciplinarian. Some also attribute the soldiers' choice to the fact that he had a son, though Priscus too had a son, for an inscription in Philippopolis is dedicated to Priscus and his anonymous offspring. Another inscription in a small square temple in Philippopolis is dedicated to his wife, Tryphoniana.[20]

Philip returned the devotion of Priscus, and made him an equal with the emperor and empress in an inscription of AD 247 in Philippopolis.[21] He appointed Priscus first to the Syrian command[22] and then made him 'Rector orientis', virtually the emperor of the East. Priscus's severity in exacting taxes (in part necessary because of Philip's excessive expenditure and the heavy tribute to the Persians), was said to have been the cause of the revolt of Jotapianus in Syria.[23] Priscus remained faithful to the last. At the end of Philip's reign, when the stability of the regime was threatened, Antioch, the capital of the eastern half of the empire and the residence of Priscus, solemnly proclaimed its allegiance to the Arab dynasty.[24] His absence from the millennium celebration of Rome has been taken by some as evidence of Priscus having been deliberately kept away[25], but in fact he had died in AD 248.[26]

Philip's hopes for the future were concentrated on his son, the young Philip. It is not difficult to imagine the thrill and joy of the people of the Hauran when Philip, his son and his wife visited his old home. The pride of the Hauranis is understandable – former subjects, more recently Roman citizens, one of their own had now become emperor of all the Romans. The young Julius Severus Philippus became an object of adulation. Born in AD 237 during the reign of Maximinus, he was seven years old on his father's accession. His father named him Caesar, with the title of 'Sabastos', a title borne by Geta, the second son of Septimius Severus,[27] showing Philip's attachment to the Severan dynasty (Septimius Severus having named his son Antoninus (Caracalla) Caesar when he was nine years old). In the fourth year of Philip's reign the Senate confirmed the young Philip as Augustus and Pontifex Maximus, with powers equal to his father's.[28] An inscription at Philippopolis, contemporaneous with the foundation of the city in AD 244, confirms the year the year that the younger Philip was made Caesar.[29]

Again following the practice of Septimius Severus, from the beginning of his reign Philip published his decrees in the joint names of himself and the Caesar.[30] The 12-year-old co-emperor did not have much of a chance, for after the murder of his father by the agents of Decius in Borea, he was assassinated in his mother's arms by the Praetorian guards in whose protection he had been left.[31]

The new empress, Marcia Otacilia Severa, was married to Philip in AD 234. Her name shows that she came from a family favoured by Septimius Severus.[32] She is known chiefly for her Christianity and for Origen's letter to her.[33] Otacilia admired and felt close to the Severan empresses, had as many honours as they and bore the same titles as Julia Domna, Maesa and Mamaea.[34] She was designated Sanctissima Augusta, Mater Castrorum and Exerciutus, and Mater Senatus and Patriae.[35] Her portrait on coins and some marble busts shows a face with little expression and a resemblance, from the hairstyle, to the portraits of Furia Sabina Tranquillina.[36] Many coins were struck for her in silver and bronze with her own types of Pietas, Pudicitas and Juno conservatrix.[37] The obverses show a diademed bust, the diadem being the ancient headdress of the Hellenistic kings.[38] One medal shows the empress under the sign of Pudicata, and behind her a genie holding a cornucopia. Another, minted in Antioch, portrays Otacilia with the legend 'Fecundites Temporum'.[39] Severianus, who was named commander of Maesia and Macedonia, was probably the brother of the empress.[40] Jean of Antioch claims that she had other children besides Philip, all of whom died with their father in Thrace, but this story has no foundation.[41] Whether Otacilia passed the remainder of her life in retirement, or lost her life at the same time as her husband and son, is not known.[42]

THE TEMPLE OF JUPITER – DAMASCUS
'An error in translation'

Philip's tremendous energy for building was almost all focused on Philippopolis, and on the temple of Jupiter in Damascus. On the surface, a Christian emperor building pagan temples may seem strange, but Philip's Christianity was private; he was, first and foremost, an emperor of all the Romans, and almost fanatical about preserving the Roman heritage – its traditions, religion, ceremonies and customs. Jupiter, moreover, was the protector of his house, and Philip, as emperor and as a man, had a universalism which tolerated all religions. In this he was again following Alexander Severus, who kept images of Abraham and Christ, as well as pagan heroes and teachers – Orpheus and Appollonius – in his shrine at the palace.[43]

The relationship between the temple of Jupiter and Philip was recently revealed by an error in translation from Arabic to English and Russian, and from English to French, and it is one of those rare occurrences where an error fortuitously revealed the truth.

The temple of Jupiter in Damascus, which was transformed into the Church of St John on the advent of Christianity, and subsequently the Ommayad mosque with the arrival of Islam, has been the subject of study for many historians and archaeologists. J.I. Smirnov, a Russian archaeologist of the early twentieth century, published an article concerning the Greek inscription found by the Ommayad caliph Al-Walid in the eighth century while he was enlarging the mosque and incorporating it into the remaining parts of the Church of St John. Smirnov followed the account and the English translation of the inscription contained in Guy le Strange's book *Palestine under the Moslems* (1890). Le Strange had translated the story from the Arab historian Yaqût.[44] According to Yaqût, the caliph ordered the workers to search for the ancient foundations of the original building (the Roman temple), until they reached moisture. They dug until they found a gate over which was a slab of granite, bearing an inscription in Greek. The inscription was translated into Arabic at the request of the Ommayad caliph and was included by Yaqût in his *Dictionary of Cities*. Le Strange translated the inscription from Arabic into English with one error. Canard, in 1945, published an article based on the translation of le Strange, used by Smirnov, and translated the inscription into French with the same error.[45] York, in 1972, translated the French version back into English, still containing the error, and Peachin did likewise in 1991. Part of the English translation from Canard's French version reads as follows: 'As the world has been created, it being granted that there is an uninterrupted series of indications that the world has been created, it is necessary that there should have been a creator of all things, as the man of the two teeth and the two jaws has said, it is necessary that the creator be adored. The lover of horses has ordered the building of this temple of his own money. If he who would enter this temple judge it fitting to mention the builder, let him do so.'[46]

The 'lover of horses' or *'l'amateur de chevaux'* in the English and French versions is the literal translation of 'Philippus' in the original Greek – and thus, Philip the Arab, from the etymology of his Greek name, was thought to have been one of the builders of the temple of Jupiter. The original Arabic text, however, reads 'lover of charity', (*muhib el khair* instead of *muhib el khail*),[47] the Arabic letter R having been misread for the letter L in 1890 by le Strange, on whose text all later studies were based. Errors of this sort, involving secondary sources are fairly common, but the irony in this case was that, despite the error, the interpretation fitted the facts! For Philip was indeed most probably one of the builders of the temple for the following reasons: Jupiter was the protector of Philip, and since he had elevated Damascus to colonial rank during his visit while returning from the Persian war, he probably wanted to make a gesture towards a neighbouring city which he must have known well in his youth, and the enlargement of the temple would have been a highly appropriate act; Damascus coins of the period show one or three temples;[48] the Sibylline oracle speaks of Philip's building activities in Arabia and, although Damascus was not in the Arabian province, it was nearby. Supporting this idea, Smirnov points out that the architectural forms and ornamentation of what remains of the temple indicate the third century rather than the second.[49] Dussaud has established that the temple was built in the second half of the third century and that work began either under Septimius Severus (193-211) or under Caracalla (211-217), and that construction continued throughout the third century, during Philip's reign. It is certainly logical to believe that Philip would have continued the work of the Severan emperors, and taking all aspects together, there would seem to be little doubt as to Philip's role in the building of the temple.[50]

A CITY IN ARABIA – PHILIPPOPOLIS

'Julius Philip Arab Traconitis came to Rome after he founded the city of Philippopolis' says Aurelius Victor,[51] implying that it was a priority for the emperor before he set foot in Rome. In a sense, Philip was aware that he was alien to Rome, and he wanted to tell the world that he was proud of his origins. He ordered the building of the city in the shortest time possible, with only four years before the millennium of Rome. Begun in AD 244, the work was scheduled for completion in April 248. It gathered together engineers, masons, craftsmen and artists from Asia Minor and the eastern provinces – the Hellenistic part of the empire and from North Africa and Rome.

The city was founded on the village known by the modern name of Shahba. The ancient name is not known for certain,[52] but one possibility is that it was the village of Boureké, known in the fourth century as Borekasabon. The ending 'sabon' suggests a connection with the Yemenite tribes, migrants from the ancient kingdom of Saba.[53] The modern Arabic name of Shahba could, in these terms, be a distortion of the old Arabic name of Saba.

The city was constructed with a high proportion of public monuments in relation to the few inhabitants of the old village of Shahba, for Philip did not bring new settlers to the city. It therefore had an artificial character, in the sense that it was not tied to an increase in population or real human need. The builders, in one stroke, transformed a village into an imperial city.[54]

Roman reaction to the building of the city is best seen in the XIII Sibylline oracle, which rages against the cities of Arabia and their preferential treatment by Philip.[55] The cities of the Decapolis began boasting of their heritage and advantages, to keep pace with the recent cities of Arabia - Petra and Bosra – both given the rank of metropolis, and Philippopolis to which Philip gave the title of colony.[56] The hostility reached a peak. A proud city like Antioch must have been incensed at the favour shown to the new city, which can be clearly seen in the writing of the authors of the Sibylline oracle who lived there: 'Now be adorned cities of Arabia with temples and stadia and market places... and a splendidly shining wealth and images of gold and silver and ivory, and most of all Bosra, you being permanently among them in all astrology and Philippoplis, so that you will come to grief. The resounding spheres of the Zodiac circle will not protect you, not the ram, the bull, the gemini, nor as many ascendant stars as appear with them in heaven, alas, you will have placed great trust in them, by the time your day shall finally come.'[57] From which we can gather that the city must have been luxurious, and given to the science of the stars. As to the attack on astrology, some think it was because the city was Christian. The authors of the thirteenth oracle were pagans, members of the upper class, who were ambivalent towards Philip, and resented the wealth poured into the cities of Arabia at the expense of the old Hellenistic towns of Syria. The reference to astrology is a reflection of an imperial building programme, in which astral imagery may have played a major part.[58]

The new city, founded in AD 244, lay at the edge of Leja, near the western end of Djebel Druze. Uniquely in Syria, it is typically Roman.[59] The plan is almost square, its walls aligned with the cardinal points, and presents us with a walled city with monumental triple gateways set into the middle of each of the four sides, a Roman-style central tetrapylon, baths modelled on Roman ones, a theatre, a palace complex and an aqueduct. The gates were linked to the principal Roman roads of the region.[60]

Two main streets, 26 feet wide, were paved with basalt blocks set diagonally and bordered by porticoes of rough unchanneled ionic columns. The two streets met in the civic centre with a tetrapylon. A high arched aqueduct brought water from a spring 12 miles away and ended in a water tower.[61] The Exedra, half a hexagon and trapezoidal, with walls of polished basalt, dominated the town and took the place of the Capitol in a Roman colony. As the main monument of the public plaza, it proclaimed the glory of Philip and legitimised his dynasty. Inscriptions and statues of the principal members of the family were scattered all over the Exedra. The building was closed from the back, but two sides were accessible from the front by means of a paved esplanade.[62] At the foot of the stairs the plaza had the proportions of a Roman forum. In the middle of the Exedra was a half-vaulted apse, in which was probably placed a colossal statue of Philip, but of which no trace remains. It probably had astrological connotations. On the terrace were round and rectangular niches. The Exedrda is a late development of a sanctuary, popular in the region; there are three such monuments in the Hauran, one of them bearing the inscription in Greek 'Ιερα καληβη' – sacred heights. South of the Exedra was the Philippeion, the mausoleum consecrated to the divine Marinus. It had pilasters at the corners, a corniche and Ionic capitals. In one of the southern niches, stairs climbed to the roof. In another were placed dedicatory inscriptions. One of the inscriptions is to Philip and his son, and to Julius Priscus and his wife Tryphoniana: another is to the two Philips, Otacilia Severa and Julius Priscus. A Latin inscription is dedicated to Priscus and his son by a Julius Malchos.[63] West of the civic centre stood a hexastyle temple on a terrace. Its ground plan consisted of a back wall, broken by a diagonal line with three niches, an apse and Corinthian columns.

Close to the water tower were baths, which were discovered in 1970. The exterior was of tufa and the interior was lined with slabs of polished marble and alabaster; the vaults were of fired brick, plastered and painted. Butler has claimed that the construction of the baths was superior to that of the baths of Rome.[64]

Fragments of a portrait of the emperor, fragments

from a group effigy of Philip, Otacilia and the young Philip, and statues larger than life-size were found scattered among the principal public monuments in Shahba. Among them too was a head of Philip, crowned with laurel, with traces of red paint. The eyes are barely open and the face shows an aquiline nose reminiscent of the portrait bust in the Vatican Museum.[65] In one room a ceramic statute of Philip was found. The statue is cuirassed, with the right foot resting on the trunk of a palm. The right hand holds a lance or sceptre and the emperor is depicted as making a libation (lustratio), purification of the army and their chief for the spilt blood.[66]

The theatre was small and was constructed in a short space of time, and if the monuments of Philippoplis are seen as faithful to tradition, the theatre shows original characteristics in its lack of ornamentation. This is a feature of the third century when, with the weakening and decline of the classical spirit all over the Roman world, the taste for decoration was lost. It departs from the canons of Antonine architecture in the Hauran, and does not conform in its proportions to the Roman theatres generally. Instead, the proportions correspond to a harmony of numbers and were determined purely by topography. In the third century, especially in the Orient, fewer theatres were constructed than in the second.

The construction at Philippopolis utilized local labour, a fitting outlet for local talent. Philip selected his architects from the Orient. The Greek letters on the blocks show that the workers came from the Hellenized part of the empire.[67] As the area was not wealthy, it must be assumed that the emperor paid the costs for all the buildings – palace, temple, Exedra, baths and theatre. He may also have paid for the city walls, the paved streets and the great tetrapylon at the city's centre. The expenses of the architects and the building materials, as well as the speed of construction, suggest an enormous outlay.[68] Victor[69] speaks of the extravagance of Philip, as does the Sibylline oracle. The neighbouring areas probably bore some of the costs.

The mosaic of Aiôn, a main feature of Philipppoplis, had an eye on the millennium celebration. It depicts Aiôn in a form that closely resembles Philip, and implies the assimilation of the emperor with external time (Aeternitas) which governs the world. It is an allegory of universal happiness and renewal, personified by the seasons, and related to the mythology of Rome elaborated for the celebrations.[70]

Aiôn was conceived of, since the time of Augustus, as governor of the world and perpetual creator of natural phenomena, and the liaison of eternity with the emperor. This presupposes a system which the continuity of a dynasty was necessary for universal domination. Under Hadrian, the emblems of the golden age (Saeculum Aureum) were identified with Aiôn. The millennium of Rome offered Philip many opportunities from which he could profit: it consolidated his dynasty and it re-established order in the empire. Nobody was better placed than he, therefore, to represent Aiôn. The idea of universal power, exercised by a god, was based on ancient Egyptian beliefs and was passed on to the Ptolemies. Philip paid great attention to Egyptian religion, more so than other emperors, as is clearly shown from his Alexandrian coins.[71]

The mosaic itself has twenty-four figures, with Greek inscriptions and three themes with Aiôn, Ge and Prometheus in one composition. Aiôn is seated on the left, with the four seasons behind him. In the centre, Ge sits on the earth surrounded by the four Karpoi. In the second row Georgia is reclining on a hill and behind her Triplotemus, the young God of Elusis, is leading an ox. On the right, Prometheus is modelling a human figure, while Aphrodite (Venus) stands beside him watching as the mother of the Romans his work. Behind him, Hermès is holding Psyche in his right arm. From the top corners of the mosaic four winds blow, Notos and Euros on the left, Zéphyre and Borée on the right. In the centre stand two small-winged geni, and the Dorsoi water the earth from urns. [72]

The mosaic reflects a purely Greek spirit, the allegorical and mythical Greek themes being familiar to cultivated circles in the provinces, as in Rome, in the third century.[73] Will has observed a Syrian colouration of the veil of Ge, borrowed from Atargais.[74] Aeternitas is linked with Aiôn, and Renovatis (renewal) with the seasons. Abudantia, Felicitas, and Fecundates find their expression in the central group.

Aiôn is represented as a robust man, his torso naked, legs covered with a cloak pinned to the left shoulder. The cloak, a paludamentum, is portrayed on many imperial statues. The royal band on the head indicates an emperor of the third century. The features are peculiar to Philip – the same round haircut and short beard as in his other portraits. The mosaic attests the assimilation of Philip with Aiôn, in the city that bears his name, and where the cult of his ancestors is celebrated. It illustrates themes of imperial propaganda, the goodness of the earth, the imperial virtues from Augustus to Philip, associated with the millennium celebrations of Rome.[75]

Other mosaics of Philippopolis were uncovered by Dunand. The 'Mosaic of the Four Seasons', discovered in 1938 and still unpublished, shows Ge (the Earth) offering the gifts of the Seasons to Bacchus and Ariadne, this scene being enclosed in a border of alternating yellow-ochre and red-ochre scrolls. A group of mosaic pavements had already been uncovered by Dunand in 1925, three of them depicting mythological scenes. These belonged to a building north-east of the main Roman road that bisected the city from east to west. Two geometric mosaic floors were found in another house, between the north gate and the tetrapylon.[76]

THE IMPACT OF PHILIPPOPOLIS

Feverish activity characterized the building of Philippopolis, with the aim of completing it before the celebration of Rome's millennium. Launched in AD 244 upon Philip's accession, the work was planned for completion in April 248 on the day of the celebration. The impact of the work of skilled masons, engineers, architects, sculptors, artists, craftsmen and mosaicists, who had been recruited from the Hellenistic East and North Africa and of the masons and engineers from Rome, was felt all over the Orient. Only recently have archaeological excavations and surveys of ancient sites in Syria begun to yield information indicating the depth of their influence over building programmes both in towns and villages. Surveys in the Syrian Golan have demonstrated that such influence percolated the countryside, reaching even small agricultural villages. A guard tower erected on the summit of the hill overlooking the village of Er-Ramthaniyye, protected it and its agricultural lands from nomadic incursions, which were frequent during the third century AD. Its masonry, of poorly squared blocks and mortar, suggests that it was built during the reign of Philip the Arab. This distinct stone blocks-and-mortar technique was imported into the eastern Roman Empire by craftsmen specially brought from Rome at the command of Philip to reconstruct his birthplace in the Roman style. This characteristic building technique has also been recognized at Na'aran on the eastern branch of the Via Maris which linked Tiberius to Damascus. A spring, with a Roman bath-house built of stone blocks and mortar, served the fortress-like mansion, or staging post, which crowned the summit of the hill and was integrated into the official system of the cursus publicus, the Imperial Post.[77]

MOSAICS FROM NABLUS AND MARIAMIN (NEAR HAMA)

A polychrome mosaic pavement was discovered in Nablus in 1973, forming the northern part of the floor of a long hall. Its features are shared by two mosaics depicting scroll borders with central emblema in Mariamin and Philippopolis. The dating of the Mariamin pavement is based on style, as well as on the similarity between the hairstyles of the female musicians in the emblema and that of the Empress Otacilia Severa as portrayed in sculpture and on coins. The Nablus pavement and the 'Mosaic of the Four Seasons' in Philippopolis exhibit numerous similar features including meticulous craftsmanship, the theme of the hunt, and the black ground of the border. Comparative stylistic analysis corroborates the dating from the Nablus pavement to the middle or third quarter of the third century on epigraphic and technical grounds.

Due to the total absence of mosaic pavements during the reign of Philip the Arab both in the Hauran and in the Nablus area, the hypothesis may be put forward that mosaicists from Rome and North Africa were brought to these eastern regions where they established temporary or permanent workshops.[78]

Philip not only raised the political and economic fortunes of the east, he also provided a great impetus to the arts, enabling the Syro-Palestinian province and the province of Arabia to become areas of flourishing artistic development.

The ruins of the city of Philippopolis (Shahba) seen *(left)* in a 19th century drawing, and *(right)* the same view in a contemporary photograph. *Below,* detail of a third century mosaic discovered in Shahba.

CHAPTER SIX

EMPEROR IN ROME

THE PEACEFUL YEARS

Rome was forlorn, for its emperor had been absent for about two years. The Romans were restless. Life was without lustre, drab and dull, for they were deprived of the imperial court which was the pivot of the life of the city, the theatre in which life achieved meaning. They missed the processions, the pageants, the banquets, the flow of visiting client kings with their outrageous garments and flashing jewels. They missed the gossip about the imperial family, an exercise in which all classes of Romans indulged, prying into their private lives for hidden vices – or, where none were to be found, inventing them.

Philip the Arab took his time returning to Rome. More than a year had passed since his elevation to the purple, and he was still on the road. To some, it seemed the emperor hesitated before entering Rome, because he was an alien. To others, he wanted to establish himself securely before he came to the city. The Romans were spoilt, they expected life to provide them with pleasure and the emperor to provide them with amusement, spectacle, theatricals, gladiatorial contests and games. None were more impatient than the plebs. They could expect a donation at the beginning of any reign, but from Philip they expected more, for rumours circulated that he was free with money. The senators, more sedate, were already seduced by the moderation and respect he showed in his missives and despatches. They felt relatively secure as, a year into Philip's reign, none of Gordian's partisans in the Senate, nor the officials who had served under him, had been harmed. The aristocracy bided their time; those clans who were partisans of the Severi had great expectations of Philip, who was somehow linked to them, and those who were Gordian partisans appreciated his devotion to the dead emperor, for was he not carrying his remains all the way to Rome, and, rumour had it, intended to ask the Senate for Gordian's deification?

Both the aristocracy and the plebs looked forward to the beginning of a new regime, to the coming of the beautiful Empress Otacilia, and they wanted to obliterate the years of suffering under a barbarian emperor and overcome their grief for the dead boy emperor. They were jealous of all the cities in Syria, Asia Minor and Thrace in which Philip had lingered and which, by virtue of his presence, became capitals of the empire. Those in the know were aware that, although Philip had been selected and elevated by the army, he was of the senatorial party. The rift between the army and the Senate had been accentuated after the revolt of North Africa against Maximinus, which had been headed by the imperial official Gordian, a venerable old man, and grandfather (or great uncle) of the young Gordian III.

The Senate was a living symbol of former glories and the senators were rich and powerful. Although they were not allowed to engage in commerce (as it was considered demeaning) they owned land throughout the empire and were exempt from liturgies (compulsory financial contributions). Philip treated them with courtesy and won them over with his reasonableness, maintaining cordial relations with them throughout his life.[1]

There was a large gap, however, between the

CHAPTER SIX

soldiers and the Senate. The senators and members of the prosperous élite from Italy did not have adequate military training; their role was limited to traditional honours and functions. The troops, on the other hand, consisted mainly of Romanised peasants and children of soldiers from border areas. They were suspicious of the literary-minded senators and called them effeminate. There was also a lack of discipline on the northern and eastern frontiers for since the time of Septimius Severus soldiers from the lower ranks had been promoted to the officer class. Thus in the third century a savage struggle developed within the empire between the party of the senators and the élite, characterized by their devotion to Roman tradition, and the military party (viri militaris) – mainly Rhine and Danube peasants from whom the army was increasingly recruited. The peasants wished to dispose of the rich and impede the spread of Christianity. In short, Rome was the battleground, but Philip, himself a soldier, constantly asserted that his regime followed the traditions and authority of the Roman past.[2]

So, almost a year after his accession to the purple, at the age of forty-one, Marcus Julius Verus Philippus, Imperator Caesar, Pius Felix, Invictus Augustus, Persicus and Parthicus Maximus,[3] Carpicus Maximus, and Germanicus Maximus,[4] known as Philip the Arab, the first and last Arab to occupy the imperial throne, finally arrived in Rome.

Philip's traditionalism is most clearly seen in his laws and his coinage. He allowed the imperial mints to continue the coins in current usage, but in his numismatic legends and inscriptions he placed a strong emphasis on what he believed to be his destiny, the foundation of a new dynasty,[5] explaining perhaps why his wife and son figure so prominently on the coinage.

In Rome, Philip had a sense of what was wrong and

a strong urge to rectify matters. He demonstrated his belief in constitutional government, and his reign was most effective on a judicial level. One of his first acts in Rome was to grant a general amnesty in an attempt to reconcile the various factions. The amnesty covered those exiled to remote areas and states, 'Our general forgiveness has bestowed a return for exiles, but it has not restored the places taken away from the military, not does it save their reputation unharmed and unspotted.' The reservation was limited to military who had been exiled for political or religious reasons by Maximinus and Timesitheus.

Philip was interested in law and legislation; his pronouncements have an important place in the Codex Justinianus. He was at his best in matters involving theft, labour and offences involving property. He acted to protect civil rights, and intervened against injustices of the treasury administration.[6] He took measures to suppress male prostitution and closed brothels, even though they were authorized and paid taxes. Measures prompted, according to Victor, by Philip's walking through the streets and seeing in front of a brothel a young prostitute who looked like his son.[7]

Certain of Philip's laws had implications for Christianity; the prohibition of homosexuality and castration, the curbing of resources for articulate groups generally hostile to Christianity, and the protection of the rights of families and religious groups to control their cemeteries.[8] To improve administration, he created a new province, Caria-Phrygia, out of the old province of Asia.[9]

Of his public works in Rome only one is known, a reservoir in the west of Rome.[10] He was very active in road building, not only in Italy but in the Balkans, North Africa and Cappadocia.[11]

Philip has been accused of being a spendthrift, and his reign was certainly one of massive expenditure.

Not only was there the tribute of 500,000 denarii to the Persians, but also the tribute to the Goths, both considerable drains on the treasury, although the latter payment was stopped by Philip in AD 248.

Aurelius Victor speaks of Philip's extravagance in the building of Philippopolis. To add to these expenses were the donations to the people of Rome, the first on his arrival in Rome at the end of AD 244, with two further donations – an above average figure for the five years of his reign.[12]

The expenditure on the lavish millennium celebration must have been without precedent. Some expenses were met by gathering overdue taxes (with no exemptions), the number of tax-payers boosted by the return of exiles under the amnesty. But taxes were a thorn in Philip's flesh. He had inaugurated his reign with a reduction of tax arrears: a series of coins and medallions bear the legend 'Acquitas Augusti' and 'Acquitas Publica', but this benevolence did not last, and rather than introduce a new tax, he resorted to gathering overdue taxes with severity.[13] There were inherent inequalities in the tax system, with areas such as the Rhine and various Danubian and Balkan provinces hardly paying any tax, while the eastern provinces were heavily taxed, a fact with was to lead to revolts.[14]

Philip did not waive legal claims – no father was exempt because his son was a prisoner of war. Nor were poets immune from taxation.[15] Heavy taxation had long been a major problem in the empire, and not only for individuals. By the early third century the provincial cities of the empire were taxed to provide golden crowns for the heads of emperors, and crowns for military victories. These cities had guilds of merchants and artisans known for certain products. In the eastern provinces, for example, Tarsus was known for fine linens, Sidon for cast bronzes, Gaza for wine, Damascus for sword-making and Daphne, a suburb of Antioch, for prostitution![16]

In the cities, municipal counsellors (Decurions) were expected to pay generously for the construction of temples, baths, fountains, gates and theatres, and also for free bread and free wine. Voluntary contributions became compulsory (liturgies) and cities were obliged to pay for games and for repairs to public buildings. Tax collectors were appointed: if they could not gather the full amount requested, their own estates were seized and their property ceded to the State. Sons of Decurions were compelled to take honorary positions and to fulfil public duties within their fathers' communities.[17]

Egypt was a particular problem. The collection and transport of Egyptian taxes was essential for Rome, but Egypt was in no condition to be milked further. The crop yield had fallen, and it could only supply one third of the corn needed by Rome. But Philip was hard pressed; the cost of the Egyptian administration seemed to him inflated and he created a special commission to supervise a general reform. He established a financial official (Rationalis) with a special assistant, equal in rank to the Prefect. He set out to achieve higher productivity by extending the cultivation, remodelling the apparatus of collection and transport, and revitalizing the civil service. The authority fixed the total sum to be collected, and lesser officials raised the sum from the tax-payers of the area. But Philip's attempts to revive Egypt had no lasting success.[18] His reforms were midway between those of Septimius Severus and Diocletian, and all failed.

Initially, Philip did not debase the currency, but by AD 246/7 he was obliged to authorize the striking of a new, lighter, version of aurus, and the majority of coins issued to celebrate the millennium were debased sestertii and antoniniani.[19]

The most serious problem facing Philip was military anarchy – a bitter problem for a soldier-emperor and former Praetorian prefect. He turned to the Senate and the bourgeoisie for help in enforcing his measures for military reform, but they failed him. He could not ignore the fact that the army had become the real master and 'did not love work or fighting but enjoyed robbing and pillaging their fellow citizens'. He achieved temporary mastery at the start of his reign by giving them large donations and enforcing strict discipline. But when he began to economize so that 'their covetous desires were not whetted',[20] made them build roads in peacetime, and issued so few coins with military legends, the army retaliated. By the end of his reign, the eastern and western parts of the empire were crippled by revolt.

His efforts towards military reform consisted firstly of reviving the system of fortified borders in Dacia, and secondly the introduction of two high command posts, (praetorians) in the Danube and the eastern provinces. Both were disastrous. His brother Priscus, through his severity in gathering taxes, inspired two revolts in the East, and the senator Decius, to whom he gave the command of the Danube, betrayed him.

Philip stationed permanent vexilletrones, drawn from the frontier regions, in the north of Italy to assure its defence and added a mint at Viminacium to ensure the pay of the army in the region.[22]

The civil service also presented Philip with problems. Civil servants oppressed the poor. Some officials had been born into slavery, and on receiving their freedom, accumulated power and wealth. They exploited the farmers, some of whom turned to robbery.

Much as he tried, except for short periods Philip could not improve the temper of the army, which remained arrogant and mercenary. But for all his good intentions, Philip could not lighten the tax burden, lift the liturgies, nor could he keep officials and soldiers from oppressing the poor.[23]

Philip's reign is known for the abundance of his coins, especially during AD 247, the year of his triumph.²⁴ The Sun-god (Sol) occupied a special place in the pantheon of Philip and his family. A coin of his son has the legend 'νευς Ηηλιος' (the new sun). Luna, the Moon, too, was important and is represented on coins by the empress wearing a diadem and standing on a crescent.²⁵

Apollo and Diana, who replaced Sol and Luna in the third century, also appear on Philip's coins. All three members of the family frequently appear, one on the obverse, the others on the reverse. The labels are traditional: Concordia, Felicitas and Pietas, Philip and Otacilia were the earthly personification of Sol and Luna, and through Pietas, were in contact with the deities. The prince, in the metaphor of the neo-Pythagoreans, was an eagle, the only creature to look at the sun without being blinded. In this world picture, with Pythagoriean, oriental, stoic and platonic influences, the prince was a second Hercules, a personification of Jupiter and Sol Invictus, and Philip, as guarantor of a new era, depicted Jupiter his protector. As a small concession to the oriental deities, the goddess Minerva, the Roman interpretation of Allat, the Arabian goddess, is depicted on some coins with her foot on a helmet.²⁶

Philip's outward gentleness hid an iron control, and, according to the sophist Nicagoras, 'whatever the pleasures that dominate men... the emperor is slave to none of them... every kind of self restraint which is praised among men is credible when it is ascribed to this man alone, who is much in control of his desire for food, for sexual satisfaction or for other pleasures.'²⁷

AN IDEAL KING (EIS BASILIA)

The great Athenian sophist, Nicagoras, Ambassador of Athens, Herald of the Eleusinian Temple and a prominent member of an intellectual group in Athens, presented an address to the emperor Philip, which is preserved in the corpus of Aelius Aristides (Orations) identified in 1918 as an encomium of Philip the Arab.[28]

The oration was delivered at the end of the year AD 247, on the return of Philip to Rome after he had defeated the Qadi in 245/6 and driven out the Carpi, for which he received the titles of Carpicus Maximus and Germanicus Maximus,[29] and his son had been declared Augustus by the Senate. The empire had seen a relatively long period of peace, for by that date Philip had ruled successfully for three years.

The oration describes him as gentle, and states that he respected everyone and committed no vicious acts on gaining the throne,[30] that he had mastered the essentials of good education and that he was one whose character embraced every form of excellence. 'If to be a phil-hellene,' the ambassador of Athens continues, 'is a fine thing, then kingly praise certainly befits this emperor, for his is a phil-hellene.'[31]

Nicagoras, in his address, describes the sorry state of the empire in crisis: 'When the empire was tossing as in a great storm or earthquake... foundering like a ship being carried off to the end of the earth... [Philip] rather as the most experiences of emperors and one of superior intelligence, checked and stopped the rush in that direction, brought her back and secured the anchor – what man has given evidence of justice, what man of clemency, what man of any other virtue that is comparable in degree and kind to the example provided by this emperor.' He continues, 'Having as sharp an eye for what is just... he did nothing that went beyond the limits of that virtue. He made it the basis of his mercy... that the most exacting justice was tantamount to the most genuine democracy.'[32]

'He liberated all who were cowering in subjection

and enslaved by fear. There were many spies circulated in all the cities. The liberty to think and speak openly had been destroyed. From this fear he delivered and freed the souls of all men, restoring to them their liberty whole and entire. . . but he showed that it is possible for a private individual to remain unchanged when he became emperor. . .prior to the throne he proved to be such a good man that he rightly was deemed worthy of the office. He came to the throne without war or murder.' [33]

It is worth noting that Nicagoras stresses Philip's virtues before he came to the throne. Alluding to his career as a military officer and Praetorian prefect, Nicagoras says, 'He was of great assistance to the empire before he assumed power.' He continues, 'His rule is described as based on all the stoic virtues, his government moderate and respectful of the Senate[34]. . . He passed laws against homosexuality and castration, protected civil rights and provided for public works.' Philip's reign was a blessing, according to the Athenian ambassador. 'From the time when divine providence which disposes and directs all things, placed on the throne the most just and God-fearing of emperors.'[35]

There is one point in the oration that does not fit Philip, for the oration speaks of succession on the principle of selection and contradicts Philip's intention of forming a dynasty. The oration does not mention his origin, for according to de Blois, his origin was a weak point.

Nicagoras paints a picture of an ideal emperor and government, and such a rhetorical panegyric would not have been dedicated to Philip unless his administration had indeed indicated an honest, if not entirely successful, attempt to govern Rome on statesman-like principles.[36] Philip is compared to Marcus Aurelius[37] and although there may be exaggeration in the characterization of Philip and a

CHAPTER SIX

certain idealization of his character, it expresses nonetheless the ideas of an emperor as perceived by the educated classes of the time. The oration portrays a just ruler equipped with stoic virtues, a benevolent prince.

We learn from 'Eis Basilea' that Philip was a cultivated man, a philhellene, who probably enjoyed the company of the Sophists in Rome, among whom were two Arabs – Maior, who prepared 13 books on Steseis (a sect of philosophy) during Philip's reign[38] and Zethus, who was one of the companions of Plotinus, the Neoplatonist.[39] Porphyry, a student, companion and biographer of Plotinus, was probably also an Arab, for his original name was Malik.[40]

As for Plotinus, we know that he came to Rome from Antioch at the age of forty, when Philip was emperor. His acquaintance with Philip went back to the Persian war, when he was probably a comitatus, or member of the personal train of the emperor Gordian, and as such, was one of the inner circle of Timesitheus who gathered learned men around him. The circle would have included the other Praetorian prefect, Julius Priscus, and his brother Philip, the deputy Praetorian prefect.

It was perfectly logical, therefore, that Plotinus should go to Rome and seek a meeting with Philip. Plotinus embodied the whole range of thought and his life was dedicated to the eternal quest for an invisible god. While in Rome, we presume that he became a member of the intellectual circle surrounding Philip, which included Nicagoras. Plotinus, we know, remained in touch with the higher circles in the Roman government long after the death of Philip. He had senators in his audience and one of them, Rogatianus, renounced his rank, his belongings and his household to join Plotinus. The emperor Gallienus (AD 253-260) and his wife Salome respected and honoured him.[41] Plotinus, like Philip, was from the east, born in Egypt at Lycopolis (Assiut), and was only a year younger than Philip. Both were highly Hellenized Orientals.

Plotinus became the greatest name in Neoplatonism, the last school of Greek philosophy, and one of the last intellectuals of the ancient world. He began the study of philosophy when he was 28 years old, and for eleven years was the student of the philosopher Ammonius Socca in Alexandria, a self-taught philosopher who wrote nothing. Origen, the Christian theologian, was also one of his students.[42] Plotinus came to reject his bodily form, and could never bear to talk about his race, his parents or his native country. He objected to sitting for painters or sculptors and said to Amelius, his chief assistant from Iturea, 'Is it not enough to have to carry the image in which nature encased us, without your requesting me to agree to leave behind me a longer lasting image of the image?'[43]

The philosophy of Plotinus is beyond the scope of this study, but his influence on Philip may be perceived from the inscription in the temple of Jupiter in Damascus. Plotinus says of the influence of the stars: 'If there was not a unique master or creator, on whom all depend, who permits each being, according to his nature to arrive at his objective [end] and to accomplish his function, in coordination with him (the creator)... to think otherwise is to destroy the nature of the world, to ignore that he has a principal and a first (primary) cause, which extends to all beings.'[44] This may be compared with the inscription from the temple of Jupiter and attributed to Philip: 'As the world has been created, it being granted there is an uninterrupted series of indications that the world has been created, it is necessary that there should have been a creator of all things... and the worship of the creator that created things.'[45]

Philip's acquaintance with Plotinus and Origen, the

two greatest thinkers of his age, both before and after he came to the throne, must have had a great influence on his universalism, his tolerance, moderation, love of justice and restraint.

It is interesting to note that in the Persian war, Mani, the 24-year-old founder of the Manichaen religion, was serving in the Persian camp, for he was close to Shapur. On the day of Shapur's coronation, Mani announced to him the word of God[46] and the birth of the Manichean religion, which swept the East to rival Christianity in the West from the third to the fifth centuries. In the opposite Roman camp was the 39-year-old Plotinus, who was hoping that after victory he would meet and learn from eastern philosophers and wise men of the east. The influence of Plotinus's Neoplatonism on Western thought has been immeasurable, so too has it been on Eastern thought, philosophy and mysticism, to such an extent that Arab historians call him the 'Greek Sheikh'.

ROME'S THOUSAND YEARS

In the third century, the empire of Rome, despite dissention within and trouble without, still represented, at least in the Roman's view, the most civilized portion of the earth. In celebrating the thousand years of their glorious city, the Romans forgot briefly the storms raging in the empire, and the emperor, in the eye of the storm, believed it to be his finest hour.

All eyes turned to Rome for the millennium of its foundation. There was a thrill of being alive for the celebrations of the greatest city on earth, ten centuries since Romulus and his band of shepherds fortified their encampment on the banks of the Tiber.[47] The Roman emperor was happy; four years of his reign had passed in relative peace, and he had just returned to Rome after his triumph on the Danube.

Rome held Dacia again, and none could complain that the emperor had done him any injustice, nor cite any act of cruelty on his part, and above all, it fell to his lot to celebrate the millennium of Rome. The celebrations were to combine the saecular games with the Jubilee on 21 April 247, for 753 BC was the traditional date of the foundation of Rome. But the event was postponed until 21st April 248 due to the emperor's absence fighting the Carpi barbarians.

The celebration was presumably presided over by the Sacred College of fifteen men (quindecembris), the keepers of the Sybilline books. No text, however, mentions the College, possibly because the date 248, correct for the millennium, was incorrect for the saecular games: the previous games had been celebrated by Septimius Severus in AD 204, which left only a 44 year interval between the two, instead of the hundred years as required.

People were persuaded they would witness a resurrection of Rome, a new era, a new cycle of eternity. The words regeneration, renewal and hope were on everyone's lips. To Philip, renewal was associated with the new dynasty he had established, and he felt he could give the gods a little assistance in shaping the forthcoming age.[48]

Roman emperors were familiar with the idea of renewal and a new age. The symbol of the 'golden age' (Saeculum Aureum) began with Hadrian and was proclaimed by Septimius Severus on his arch in Rome, and in the saecular games he held. Philip followed their example and the theme of the 'golden age' appears on his coins and medallions, and on the mosaic of Aion in Philippopolis, for the celebration of the millennium in Rome was related to the notion of 'Romae Aeternae', associated with 'renovalia' and felicitas temporum'.

The ritual was celebrated in the temple of Rome and Venus, known as 'Templum Urbis'[49] which, as the only temple of Rome in the city, played an important role in the celebration. The temple, in which Rome and Venus held equal rank, had been built in AD 137 by Hadrian in the velia, for a special ritual associated with the annual celebration of the birth of Rome. The ritual, which became a national tradition, established the firm connection between the fortunes of the time and the eternity of Rome, a belief which Hadrian spread all over the empire through the legends on coins.[50] The concept of 'eternal Rome' as a religious belief led also to the development of a 'mystique of the imperial'. Since its dedication, this special ritual had been enacted in the temple every 21st April with circuses and sacrifices to the templum urbum.

The temple played an important role until the fourth century. It upheld the Roman ideas and ideals for two centuries, and preserved the popularity of all national legends, and most emperors served it faithfully. By so doing, the sacred image of the city was maintained above that of the provinces.[51]

An extensive series of coins was struck for the celebration, in all metals, and these figured the images of Philip, his wife, and his son, and bore the legends 'Saeculares Augusi', Saculum Nouvum', Milenaria Augusti' and Romae Aeternae'. Some of the coins, which bear the legend, show a temple with six or eight columns and a statue of Jupiter or Roma in the centre. The building is probably the 'Templum Urbis' of Rome and Venus before which the celebration occurred. Other coins show a temple in a field, and behind it a sacrificial scene, others show games and sacrifices in front of a temple. Sacrifices clearly played an important role in the celebrations.

The pomp and magnificence of Philip's entertainment dazzled the eyes of the multitude: his city in Arabia was completed and in Rome the people were provided with spectacles and the distribution of bonuses which exceeded their expectations. But

Philip must have been momentarily blinded by his own self-importance and the delusion that his dynasty would last forever. Some coins struck for the occasion have the image of an aged elephant, and the legend 'Aeternatis Augg'.[52] Little did he realize that the destiny he believed in was an illusion, and that a dark shadow loomed, warning that his time had passed.

The celebration lasted three days and three nights; foreigners and slaves were forbidden on pain of death to show their faces during this exclusively Roman celebration. Thousands of torches glowed on the Campus Martius, and holy pageants were performed on the Palatine and Capitoline. Wheat, barley and beans were passed to the crowd; people danced in the field of Mars and drank much wine[53] or watched theatrical performances, gladiatorial combats and a display of rare animals. Philip employed a thousand pairs of gladiators and a whole army of exotic animals, three thousand in number, which had been assembled by Gordian for his anticipated triumph in the Persian war and his victorious return to Rome. There were leopards, rhinoceroses, horses, lions, giraffes, hippopotami, elks, tigers, hyenas, and wild asses.[54] Such bloodshed to herald in a new century of glorious history!

The emperor, as the high priest of the state religion, veiled and clad in a toga, carried out endless rituals at the altars. Along the Tiber, he burned lambs and she-goats to the fates who caused men to prosper or fail. He sacrificed white bulls to Jupiter, the patron of Rome and king of the gods, a spotless heifer to Juno, Jupiter's wife and patroness of Rome, a pregnant black sow to Mother Earth who gave the empire food or made men starve. He offered cakes and burned incense to Ilithya, goddess of the child, without whose assistance the population would decrease.[55] Twenty-seven aristocratic youths and twenty-seven virgins, their lives unpolluted by the death of either parent, chanted ancient hymns to Apollo and his sister Diana. They invoked the benediction of the gods and implored the propitious gods to favour the present and give hope for the rising generations.

For Philip, as well as providing the opportunity of inaugurating a new age, the eternity of Rome with that of his new dynasty, the millennium was also the occasion to demonstrate that his foreign origin was forgotten and that he was really a Roman.[56] It also allowed him to attract the favour of the plebs by feasts and donations.

The celebration caused a significant stir throughout the empire, for although the end of the millennium might herald the birth of a new age, it might also be associated with violent destruction and the arrival of a king from the East to finish off the Romans for good! Oracles of this sort were current and well known.[57] But the optimism and expectations were somewhat misplaced, for decay was gnawing at the heart of the empire, with Roman sovereignty on the wane. The storm was brewing, and Philip was in the eye of the storm. The magnificent festival he held was but a spark of light amid the dark forces disrupting his world, for even during the celebration his eastern troops were fighting Persia following the breaking of the treaty of AD 244. Revolts broke out in the eastern and the western provinces and, while Philip was still celebrating, three military usurpers in separate garrisons set up their own generals as emperors.[58] Frankish vanguards were approaching the Rhine, and Goths, Carpi and Vandals were crossing the Danube.[59]

The brilliance of the celebration, with its strict adherence to Roman religion, legend and tradition, aroused the admiration of some and the jealousy of others, who raged against Philip. But Philip at least had the satisfaction of having done his duty to the Roman world, as emperor, consul, and Pontifex

Maximus. The games were a pagan festival and Philip carried out his priestly and secular roles to perfection.[60]

This celebration was to be the last in the Roman world. Authors like the Roman Aurelius Victor, who a hundred years after Philip's death lamented its omission, and the Byzantine Zosimus, who in his contempt for Philip did not even mention the millennial celebration, also deplored the absence of the celebration.[61]

CHAPTER SEVEN

THE FIRST CHRISTIAN EMPEROR

"Primus de regibus Romanus Christianus fuit."
St Jerome

CHRISTIANITY TOOK root very early among the Arabs of the Fertile Crescent; they were one of the first groups in the Orient to adopt the new religion. By the first century AD[1] it had begun to spread.

The monks of the desert played a role in the conversion of the Arab nomads.[2] Eusebius, born 11 years after Philip, drew attention to the noticeable spread of Christianity among the Saracens of the desert.[3] In Bosra, the capital of the Arabian province, Christianity was attested at the beginning of the second century, if not before.[4] The conversion of the Arab Abgar VIII (AD 179-218), ruler of the kingdom of Osroeni, made him the first Christian ruler of any state in the world.

There were churches in Petra and in the desert. A monastery in the Hauran was established in AD 180. The Christian Church east of Jordan was well organized in the second and third centuries. Bosra was the ecclesiastical as well as civil metropolis of the Hauran: the town was a great centre of trade, second only in importance to Damascus, and was full of monks. The diocese had its own theology and its synod[5] and wrestled with the problems of early Christianity.[6]

Origen, a Christian theologian from Alexandria, had close connections with Christian Arabs. He was first summoned to Antioch by the Arab imperial mother of Alexander Severus, Julia Mamea, to discuss the principles of Christianity. His first visit to the Arabian province was in AD 218, at the demand of the governor of the province who wrote formal letters to the governor of Egypt and to Demetrius, bishop of Alexandria, requesting that Origen should be sent to him to discuss Christian doctrine. The governor, noticing the rapid spread of Christianity among the Arabs, wanted to inform himself about the cult, in order to be able to govern them.[7] It is possible that the adolescent Philip met Origen at that time.

Origen was summoned a second time to the Hauran, whose Arab population were being branded by orthodox theologians as heretics. The province of Arabia became known as 'Haeresium Ferax', and its bishop Beryllas, who was well-known among churchmen and who left works of great literary merit, was accused of perverting the true doctrine of the Church and, according to the Church historian Eusebius, tried to introduce ideas alien to the faith.[8] The heresy of Beryllas was based on his belief that Jesus did not pre-exist in his own form of being before he made his home among men, and had no divinity of his own, but had only the Father dwelling in him. The arguments and supplications of a number of bishops to Beryllas were to no avail, and Origen was summoned in the hope that he could deal with the situation. Origen succeeded in reforming Beryllas' unorthodox ideas and establishing him on a more acceptable doctrinal path.[9] But that was not the end of the story.

It seems it was difficult for the individualist Arabs to conform: a new group of heretics appeared on the scene, who preached that at the end of life on earth, the human soul dies and perishes with the body. Only later, with the resurrection, would it return to life. With this new crisis, a large-scale synod was convened, and Origen was invited again to instruct the Arab heretics. On his arrival, he opened a public debate and urged those who had gone astray to change their views. Meanwhile, another heresy sprang up among the Arabs, started by the 'Helksaite sect' who preached that 'to deny the truth does not matter; in case of need, the sensible man will deny it with his lips, but not in his heart.' [10] These heretics produced a book, alleging that its contents fell from heaven and that anyone who should hear it, read it and believe it would receive forgiveness for their sins. With Origen's help, this heresy was soon extinguished.

These various heresies among the Arabs, starting with that initiated by their own bishop, demonstrate not only their individualism, rebelliousness and non-conformism, but that there were great numbers of Arab Christians in the Hauran in the third century. The importance of these Christian communities in the Orient is demonstrated by the fact that the emperor Gallienus (AD 253-268), who came to the throne only four years after Philip, was obliged to abandon his father's campaign of persecution against the Christians in order to secure their support in his campaign against the Persian ruler Shapur.[11]

Philip the Arab came from Shahba, which probably had a large Christian population and, being close to Bosra, teemed with Christians, and was born a Christian.[12] His wife, too, was born a Christian. Meeting Origen during his visits to the province, must have had a great influence on Philip. Some believe that Origen was a teacher, and later a counsellor of Philip, and bequeathed to him his ideas of universalism, which make it possible for a Christian magistrate to participate in pagan worship or pagan celebrations, such as the millennium in Rome, with only a mental reservation.[13] In his reply to 'Celsus', an epicurian writing in the reign of Marcus Aurelius, who attacked the Christians as subversive and who predicted that converted Roman emperors would be captives both of the Christian creed and of external enemies of the empire, Origen stated that the emperors had not yielded to captivity; leaving open the question as to whether the Philips (father and son), in whose reign he wrote, were Christians[14] or Christians that had not yielded.

It was natural that Origen should be interested in the first Christian emperor, and that he should write to Philip and his wife, the empress Otacilia, in AD 244 while the emperor was still in the East.[15] In order to understand Philip's Christianity, however, one has to probe the teachings of Origen and their possible influence on Philip. Origen was a Greek, schooled in Greek thought, who associated himself at all times with Plato[16] and the writings of the more eminent followers of Pythagoras. He was a pupil of the Alexandrian philosopher Ammonius Sacca, the teacher of Plotinus. Origen fell out with his bishop Demetrius, and left Alexandria for Caesarea in Palestine where he set up an academy. His asceticism was so severe that he made himself a eunuch through self-emasculation, and thus could not be ordained. His output was phenomenal, but during the Christian persecution of Decius, Philip's successor, he was imprisoned and cruelly tortured. He died in 253 in Tyre.[17] Porphyry, the biographer of Plotinus, met him in AD 250 in Caesarea and violently attacked his Christian teaching.[18]

In the sixth century, almost three hundred years after his death, Origen was considered a heretic by the Church for the original controversy on desert monasticism in the late fourth century, which had led to his condemnation.[19] His method of teaching, according to a certain Theodore who wrote in AD 238 (and whom Eusebius equated with Gregoire le Thaurmaturge), is recorded as follows: he made his students read all existing texts of ancient philosophers and poets, without denying or rejecting anything save the writings of atheists. He also made his students study and familiarize themselves with other philosophers, without manifesting disdain or preference for any one school or philosophical doctrine, whether Greek or barbarian. He chose from each philosophy what he considered to be true and useful, and he advised his students not to be attached to any single philosophy, but only to respect God and his prophets. He made it possible for his students to learn all science, barbarian or Greek, mystic or political, divine or human.[20]

The teaching of Origen, therefore, represents a form of universalism, which might have influenced Philip before he became emperor, and which could explain his conduct as emperor: respect for all, open-mindedness, tolerance and reverence for Roman tradition, religion and ritual.

Most modern authors have been reluctant to accept Philip's Christianity. Their objections are many, but foremost among them is the silence in the ancient sources of the third, fourth and fifth century pagan writers, none of whom speak of his conversion or that of his wife. Most significant, perhaps, is the impressive silence of Zosimus, who vigorously hated both Arabs and Christians.[21] On the other hand, sources that refer to Philip's Christianity are Christian themselves and rely on the authority of Eusebius, a Greek Christian often called the 'Father of Ecclesiastical History', or the 'Christian Herodotus'. Eusebius was born in Palestine, 11 years after the death of Philip, and wrote in his *History of the Church*: 'There is reason to believe Philip was a Christian'.[22] In another section, he recounts Philip's passage through Antioch on his way to Rome, and his attendance at an Easter service in the guise of a penitent. The bishop of Antioch, Babylas, would not let him in until he made open confession. According to the text, 'It is said that he obeyed gladly'.[23]

This story, which circulated widely, was most probably a fiction, as it seems unthinkable that Philip would have compromised his frail authority by such a humiliating encounter.[24] It is alleged to have occurred in Antioch on Easter Day, April 244, when Babylas was indeed bishop, but it is physically impossible for Philip to have been in the city at that date, for he was only elevated to the purple between January and March 244, and could not have been in Antioch in April of the same year. Even if he were made emperor in January, we have to take into account his march with the army from Misikhe to Syria, his stops in Bosra and Damascus (possibly also in Neopolis and Ptolemias in Palestine), his visits to Heliopolis in Lebanon, and, most significantly, his long stay in Shahba to plan and order the building of Philippopolis. All of these events would have taken more than three months, making it impossible for the humiliating episode to have occurred, especially considering the almost divine honours with which the emperor is surrounded.[25]

The fact that the story circulated at all, however, reflects the bad reputation Philip had acquired in the fourth century, largely through the campaign of denigration conducted by his successor Decius.

Other Christian sources besides Eusebius confirm Philip's Christianity. Denys, bishop of Alexandria, was aware of the emperor and his son's unofficial belief, and spread this information to some of his contemporaries.[26]

Three Latin writers of the late fourth and early fifth century also affirm Philip's Christianity. St Jerome states that Philip was the first emperor to become a Christian: 'qui primus de regibus Romanus christianus fuit', but he also describes Philip in the early part of his life as a robber by profession![27]— a phrase later borrowed by Gibbon. Orisius says that

Philip was the first emperor to be a Christian, and asserts that he celebrated the millennium of Rome in honour of Christ! To support this extraordinary statement he claims that there was no procession to the Capitol, nor any sacrifice of victims according to custom.[28] The third Latin writer to use the term 'primus', first Roman emperor to adopt Christianity, was Vincent of Lerins.

Two Greek writers from Antioch, St Jean Chrystostome (AD 382) and Leontius, bishop of Antioch (AD 535) refer to Philip's Christianity, as do other Christian writers, the anonymous Constantini Imperatoris (author of Origo and Prosper Tiro), Palemius Silvus and Jordanes.[29]

A change occurred, however, when emperor Constantine made Christianity the official state religion in the fourth century. His advocates wanted him to be the first Christian emperor, which meant, of course, ignoring Philip. Eusebius, who had acknowledged Philip's Christianity in his *History of the Church*, seems to have forgotten this fact in his *Life of Constantine*, where he states that Constantine was the first Christian emperor to be baptized. Eusebius had overlooked the fact that Philip was born a Christian and therefore was baptized in his early years. Clearly one reason for ignoring Philip was to please and flatter Constantine, but there may have been another reason. Licinius, the colleague, co-emperor and brother-in-law of Constantine, claimed his descent from Philip the Arab. According to some authors, he wanted to please the Christian Constantine by claiming a Christian descent, and, in so doing, win over a large number of oriental Christians in the eastern part of the empire, where he was Augustus.[30] Licinius had been made emperor by Galerius[31] and became a colleague of Constantine, but was not in reality a Christian. Jointly with Constantine, he ratified the edict in which the emperor Galerius recognized Christianity in AD 313, known as the edict of Milan. Christianity was now religio-licita. Later, the two emperors fell out, and Licinius became Constantine's most bitter enemy: he was defeated at Chalcedon in 324.[32] The damnatio memoriae, which followed his defeat, had repercussions for the memory of Philip the Arab, his alleged ancestor.[33] Eusebius, not content with stating in his *Life of Constantine* that Constantine was the first Christian emperor to be baptized, clearly felt compelled somewhere between the first and fourth revision of his History of the Church to repeat the assertion, changing what was inconsistent with the damnatio memoriae of Licinius and his downfall.[34]

Historians who question Philip's Christianity consider the passage in Eusebius, and the letters of Origen to Philip and the empress Otacilia, as unhistorical, implying, at most, only a passing interest in Christianity on the part of Philip.

Apart from the silence of pagan authors on the subject, objections to the notion of Philip's Christianity are based on a number of aspects; the deification of his father, the appointment of Philip the younger as Pontifex Maximus[35] and the very pagan ritual with which he celebrated the millennium of Rome. Explanations for these 'unchristian' acts, however, are not difficult to find. Philip had a passionate interest in establishing his dynasty, which necessitated an impeccable background. His father, therefore, had to be enrolled among the gods, and his city, Philippopolis, had to rival older cities in maagnificence and serve as the family shrine. Roman emperors were conscious that the empire needed stability and continuity, especially in the mid-third century. Philip himself, as a military officer, had lived through crisis and upheaval[36] and, like most Romans, believed that the empire could best be served by a solid continued dynasty, the stability of which should avoid the tribulations that all too often plagued the end of a reign. It is true that he had been elevated by the soldiers, but he believed firmly in constitutional government, and respected the role of the Senate and the senatorial party. He also tried hard to curb the power of the army and to discipline them. He was conscious of the fact that after the assassination of Alexander Severus six emperors had ruled the empire and all had been killed by soldiers. It was this reality that led him to name his seven-year-old son as Caesar. Philip had gained legitimacy by the assent of the Senate and through his just and moderate rule.

That Philip followed strictly the pagan rituals and ancient rites of Roman religion, together with the holding of games, was due to his insistence that his regime should follow the traditions and authority of the Roman past. He took his responsibility as guarantor of the Roman state religion very seriously, and respected to the letter the Roman way of life. He played his rôle, one has the impression, with pleasure and enthusiasm and without constraint. Indeed, it would have been difficult for a Christian emperor in the third century to impose his religion on the state in the way Constantine was able to do more than 70 years later. He was open-minded and respected the religion of the majority, with only a mental reservation.[37] Philip was emperor of all, and Christian to himself.[38] It is hardly surprising that the pagan authors are silent on the subject of his Christianity – there was nothing to comment on. Philip showed no outward sign of his private religion. There is no record of his conversion or baptism because he was born into the religion, not converted, and already baptized. It is a reasonable assumption that if the pagan authors had detected any sign of Philip's Christianity, it would have been reported. His following of the Roman cult was above reproach. The argument against his Christianity on the grounds that he names his son

Pontifex Maximus also carries little conviction: the title continued to be used by Roman emperors after Christianity became the official state religion[39] and survives even today as the title of the Pope! Nor can the occurrence of pagan symbols on coins of Philip be used as an argument to question his faith: these symbols were purely traditional and continued to appear long after the adoption of Christianity by the State. The pagan Goddess Victory appears on the coins of Romulus Augustus, the last emperor of the West.[40]

While it is true that Christian authors were lukewarm on the advent of Constantine and erased what was favourable to Philip, the fictitious ancestor of Licinius,[41] the paradox was that it was probably Constantine himself who consecrated Philip as the first Christian emperor, and substituted the portraits of Philip for those of Hadrian on the two round medallions of the arch of Constantine.[42] However, others attribute the deification of Philip and his son to Licinius. Eutropius confirmed the consecration of Philip and his son as they were 'enrolled among the Gods'.[43]

The question of Philip's Christianity has exercised the minds of modern authors, too. The most determined opponent was Ernst Stein who, in 1918, dismissed the three Latin sources, St Jerome, Orosius and Vincent of Lerins, as having been derived from Eusebius, and the two Greek sources, Leontius and John Chrysostom, as based on rumours.[44] J.H.Neumann and John Gregg also deny his Christianity. De Blois opposes the idea that Philip was a Christian, believing that, although he might have been indulgent towards Christians, his alleged faith represents a late tradition in which Christianity was adopted to create a contrast with his successor, Decius, renowned as a persecutor of Christians. Petit describes Philip as 'favourable to Christians' as he allowed Pope Fabianus to honour the remains of his predecessor who had been exiled by Gordian III to Sardinia.⁴⁵ Parker describes Philip's Christianity, and his being the first Christian Roman emperor as gossip and unhistorical.⁴⁶ Brauer dismisses the story in Eusebius as legend.

Bowersock and Downey both refute Philip's Christianity on the grounds of his conduct as emperor and because of the silence of the pagan sources. Potter finds it difficult to believe he was ever a practising Christian because he deified his father, and was involved in the state cult of the millennium games.⁴⁷

There are many more modern authors who deny Philip's Christianity, among them Olmstead, Pohlsander, Grant and Oost. To them, Philip had an open-minded tolerance towards Christianity, the faith of the oppressed.

Paul Allard was one of the first modern authors to admit Philip's faith and in 1894 stated that he must have been Christian by 'birth'. Even before this, in 1880, Aube wrote: 'Philip's Christianity was latent and not admitted to, and he conformed easily to the religion of the majority.... One cannot deny his Christianity, reported by serious authors of the third, fourth and fifth centuries.' According to Aube, Philip was 'ambitious, perfidious and without scruples, but there is no reason to say he could not be a Christian.'⁴⁸ Henri Grégoire sees Philip as a Christian and a pacifist. Smith states: 'from Shahba came the first Christian emperor; he was at least a nominal Christian'. Daniel-Repos believes that he was a Christian in secret while maintaining the outward forms of paganism. Similarly, Petit believes that the emperor and his son were really Christians, but not officially.⁴⁹ The most ardent champion of Philip's Christianity is Irfan Shahid whose *Rome and the Arabs* provides the best modern source for the question.⁵⁰

The violent persecution of Christians after the

death of Philip, by the treacherous usurper Decius (AD 249-251), can in itself be seen as a reaction against the policies of the Christian Philip, and as evidence of his Christianity, for while it is true that Philip's Chrstianity was private, it was not secret and was known throughout the empire. This persecution raged all through the empire, and most especially in the Hauran. Evidence for the persecution is apparent from the inscriptions carved on pieces of basalt, with the words or syllables of 'Martyr', and are to be found in martyr's monuments raised by the Arabs, one in almost every village. Even the nomads raised monuments to the martyrs, and one was erected by a Phylarch, an Arab sheik.[51]

To those living in the fourth century, Philip was a Christian,[52] and this belief persisted for more than twelve centuries. Later Arab historians have affirmed Philip's Christianity:

• Ibn-Althir, who wrote early in the thirteenth century, reports: 'Philip ruled for six years and was a Christian, he left the pagan religion and had many followers, Decius killed him.'[53]

• Ibn Khaldun (late fourtenth century): 'Philip ruled for seven years, he was the cousin of Alexandra Severus and the first Christian emperor, he believed in Christ. Philippus was killed by Decius, who persecuted the Christians and killed the Patriarch in Rome. The story of the cave (El Kahf), occurred in the reign of Decius.[54] The story is known as the seven sleepers of Ephesus.' (See Epilogue.)

• El-Qualqashendi (early 15th century): 'Philippus ...ruled it is said six and nine years. His religion was Christianity. The first Christian of Roman emperors, killed by Decius who persecuted the Christians. In his day was the story of the cave'[55] (See Epilogue.)

To summarize, Philip was born a Christian in an Arab Christian community. There was therefore no need for

CHAPTER SEVEN

conversion or late baptism. The Christianity of Philip and his family was domestic and intimate: it had no official character, but although a personal affair, it was not a secret one. His tribal Arab ancestors were probably Christians at the end of the second century, if not earlier. A Christian when elevated to the purple, he maintained the state religion of Rome, respected the religion of the majority and carried out his secular and religious duties, and adhered to all the outward forms of paganism.

A tolerant and cultivated man, Philip, unlike many of his predecessors, did not engage in the pursuit of pleasure, nor in the exercise of tyranny. He was influenced by the sophists of his time, Origen the Christian theologian, and Plotinus the Neoplatonist pagan. Philip did not find it burdensome to be a Christian as man or emperor, and did not try to involve the state in his belief.[56]

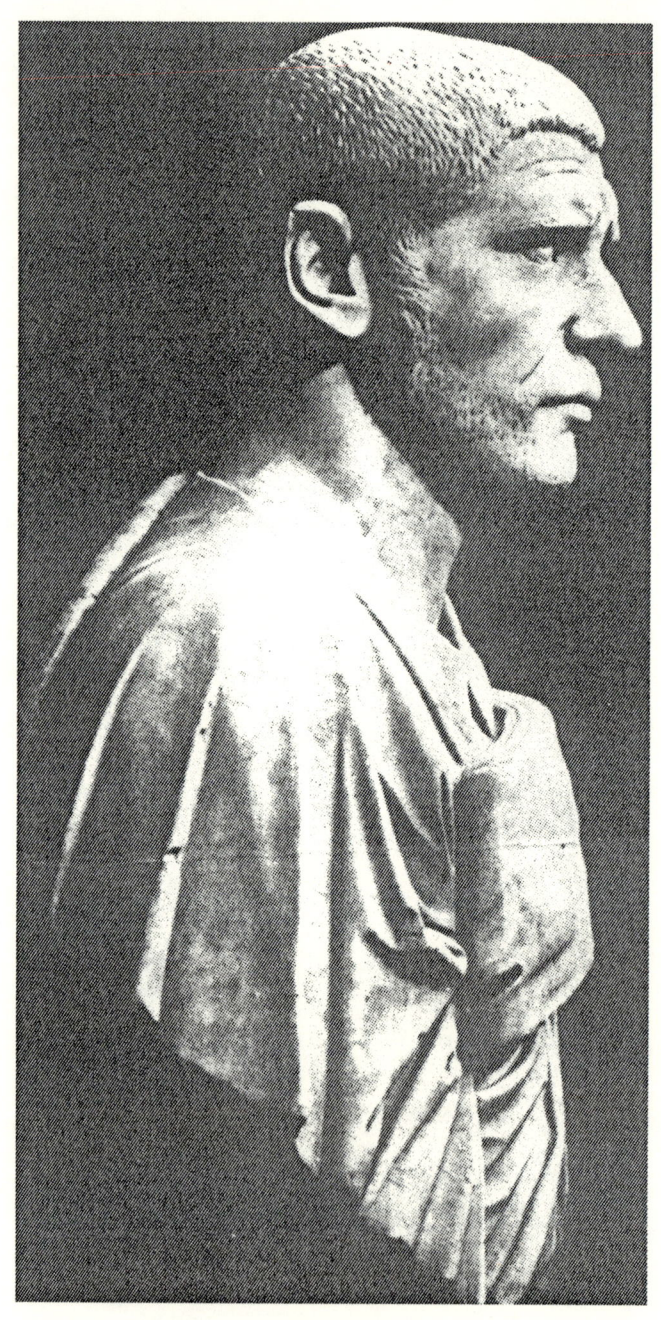

Profile of the portrait bust of Philip the Arab (Vatican Museum).

CHAPTER EIGHT

SIC TRANSIT GLORIA

CAMPAIGNS

ZONARAS EXPLAINS the delay of Philip's arrival in Rome in terms of military operations in the Danubian area.[1] The modern writer, Petit, follows this view in stating that Philip returned to Rome having vanquished the Quadi and the Carpi on the Danube.[2] These statements are contrary to the facts, for as mentioned previously he arrived in Rome early in AD 245 and campaigned against the Carpi and other barbarian tribes a little later. Certainly, we know that he was in the field in 247 and could not get back in time for the celebration of the millennium, which was postponed for a year.

The Carpi, a Thracian tribe who worked in silver and iron and built houses of brick, threatened the Roman frontiers in 244, and in 245 they crossed the Danube and spread over lower Moesia (Bulgaria). They were joined by the Quadi, a Germanic barbarian tribe who ravaged Thrace and Macedonia. Philip took the supreme command and marched to meet them in the autumn of AD 246, in the Danube area. (The cessation of Roman coinage in the afflicted areas indicates the isolation from Roman territory.) Philip defeated the Quadi in 246 and then campaigned against the Carpi who were plundering around the Danube. When the armies met, the barbarians fled to a fort, where they were besieged, then sallied forth to attack the Romans. A contingent of moors utterly crushed them. The Carpi sued for peace, which Philip granted and marched away. He returned to Rome in 247 after driving the Carpi from lower Dacia. He gave the afflicted areas the right of coinage before he returned to Rome. In Rome the Senate rewarded his success with the titles 'Carpicus Maximus' and 'Germanicus Maximus', and also confirmed his son as co-emperor with the title of Augustus. The Senate also declared his father, Marinus, divine, and bestowed honorary titles on the empress Otacilia, 'Mother of the Camp, 'Mother of Augustus' and Mother of the Senate and Fatherland'.[3]

At the time Philip was fighting on the Danubian front, he renounced the treaty with the Persian ruler Shapur, as the tribute was proving a drain on the treasury and the Romans were clamouring for the abandoned territories. Hostilities with the Persians soon began,[4] probably led by Priscus, the rector of the Orient. We have no record of the hostilities, except that Nisbis and Singara in Mesopotamia received the additional honorary title of 'Julia'[5]: whether this signifies their return to the Romans or that the title was bestowed before that is not clear. On the domestic side, Philip sent the navy to the Umbrian coast to take care of thieves and pirates who were actively raiding.[6]

Philip's last campaign in the Danube area, just before his death in AD 249, when he planned to set out for Syria to put down the revolt of Jotapianus, is dealt with on page 126.

REVOLTS

During the millennium celebration, the Franks were approaching the Rhine, the Goths, Carpi and Vandals were crossing the Danube, and the Blimmys were invading Egypt from Ethiopia.[7] A crushing wave of disasters beset Philip and the Roman Empire. Famine was a frequent phenomenon and a huge earthquake hit Italy, Greece and North Africa.[8] The bonds by which Roman power held the world were weakening, troubles brewed everywhere, wars and revolts disrupted manufacture and commerce, the monetary system was fluctuating, and there were all manner of ills and grievances.[9]

The eastern provinces, oppressed by the tribute exactions, revolted in AD 249 and proclaimed Jotapianus emperor; the Moesian and Pannonian legions on the Danube rebelled and elevated one of their officers, T. Claudius Marinus Pacatianus, of senatorial birth, to emperor. He commemorated the millennium festivities with his own coinage, with the legends 'Romae Aeter(nae): and Anno millesmo et Primo'.[10] From the evidence of the coins issued at Viminacium by Pacatianus, this revolt took place in 248 or early 249.

At the same time the Goths, emboldened by the revolt of the army and angry that Philip had cut their subsidy, violated the peace with Rome and, joined by the Carpi, invaded lower Moesia and besieged the capital Marcianopolis, a city near the Black Sea. The residents, Greeks, Italians and Thracians, resisted the barbarians and defeated two assaults. Philip was more disturbed by the revolt of the army than by the Gothic invasions. Some modern historians believe it was a Western reaction against the Oriental Arab Philip.[11] Philip's chagrin at the revolts was shattering, for these were the very troops who had raised him to the purple. It was clear to him that the root cause was the rift between the army and the constitutional government of the empire. He stood in the Senate and pleaded for help in quelling the revolts, and told the senators that if they were disappointed or displeased with him or his rule, and if they thought somebody else could do a better job, he wished them to accept his abdication.[12] There was silence in the Senate, for this man asking them to assume their responsibilities had seduced them by his cordiality and gentleness. This was Philip's greatest moment. The disasters besetting the empire were of a magnitude that compelled him to place the empire above his personal desires and to offer to renounce the throne in the interests of the empire and the people.

One senator, Decius, said that such revolts collapse quickly of their own accord. And so they did. The usurper, Pacatianus, was killed by his own troops. Philip, however, aware of the troops' hatred for their commanders (one of whom was his brother-in-law Severianus, in command of the forces in Moesia and Macedonia) called on Decius to accept the command of the legions in Moesia and Pannonia, with the stipulation that Pacatianus' supporters should be punished.[13] The revolt was soon crushed, for in early 249 Viminacium minted coins again for Philip. The soldiers, seeing Decius punish the offenders, were displeased and many defected to the barbarian camp,[14] but the majority hailed Decius as emperor as a more devious means of escaping punishment. An inscription from Vienna, from the legio Gemina, which renamed itself Daciana, is dated May 249; another inscription is dated June 249 – both indicate the first signs of the revolt. According to some versions, Decius was forced by the soldiers to become emperor, threatened by death if he refused.[15]

An unknown pretender in Gaul, Silbannacus (of whom the only record is a unique coin found in Lorraine[16]), also declared himself emperor at this time.

In the east, the Persians attacked Armenia and there were two usurpations. The revolt of Jotapianus, who was related to the ruling house of Commagene in Syria and Cappadocia, was sparked by heavy taxes, liturgies and liturgies for office (compulsory appointments). The revolt collapsed and Jotapianus was killed by his own troops,[17] but it is unclear whether this occurred under Philip or Decius.

Another usurper in Emesa, Uranius Antoninus, claimed that he was related to the Sampsigeramids, the former Arab dynasty in Emesa, and from the line of Alexander Severus, and he was more successful. It is possible that he played on Syrian resentment to the Arabian province, which was profiting under Philip, while the cities of Syria were suffering economically.[18] He remained master of a large section of Syria[19] until 253-4, during which time he issued gold coinage (aurei) at Emesa – four or five years after Philip's death. According to the XIII Sibylline oracle, this usurper defended Syria against the Persians just before he was vanquished.[20]

In the last year of Philip's reign, in the summer of 249, Alexandria saw violent unrest. This was nothing new, for there had been pogroms against the Christians in 247 and 248,[21] but this last was especially violent. It began as an anti-Christian purge, which Philip was powerless to control,[22] but turned into a general uprising against Roman authority. An Egyptian holy man, an anonymous rabble-rouser, stirred up a frenzy against the Christians, who he claimed were insulting the gods and who, he insisted, must be compelled to worship them in their temples. The gods in question were Isis and Osiris, and the temple the Serapeum. The Christians were undoubtedly singled out because of Philip's well-known interest in Christianity. The Christians of Alexandria had replaced the Jews as a focus for anti-Roman resentment.

A Christian woman was forced to the temple of the Serapeum. When she refused to worship the pagan gods, she was dragged round the city, brought back to the Serapeum and killed. Whenever Christians appeared in public, they were liable to torture and death. Dionysius, the bishop of Alexandria, fled. His account, recorded by Eusebius, described how the mob seized an old man who refused to blaspheme and how they tortured and stoned him to death.[23]

The rebels tried to prevent the corn ships from setting sail for Rome.[24] There are conflicting accounts on the sedition: one claims that the governor did not intervene, in itself a comment on the weakness of Philip in that the imperial governor could for some time defy the general principles of Roman administrations, the letter of the law and the wishes of the emperor, and demonstrates the dissolution of the bonds of empire[25] Ultimately, however, the governor was obliged to stop the attacks on Christians upon Philip's instructions.[26]

The churches were convinced that Decius' persecutions following Philip's death were a reaction against Philip's pro-Christian attitude.[27]

DEATH

The record of Philip in death, as in life, is distorted. The classical version of his death rests solely on the authority of Aurelius Victor,[28] recorded a hundred years after the event. This version glorifies Decius and can be summarised thus: Philip recognised in the Senator Decius the man who could deal with the revolt and usurpation of Marinus Pacatianus. Decius accepted reluctantly, took command of the Danubian area and succeeded in suppressing the revolt and recovering Viminacium. But the soldiers, perceiving in Decius great qualities, compelled him to assume the purple. Decius, the story goes, was loyal and sought understanding with Philip, to whom he wrote a letter promising to lay before him his imperial insignia on arrival in Rome. To prove his sincerity, he did not stamp his name or image on his coins.[29] Philip, however, did not trust him and marshalled a great army to meet his potential rival at Verona. Although outnumbered, Decius, a skilled general, was victorious and, according to this version, Philip died fighting in the front ranks, and was decapitated in Verona.[30]

The Latin sources of the fourth and sixth centuries, principally Victor and Eutropius, have the elder Philip killed at Verona, and the younger Philip killed in Rome. The emperor had left his son under the guardianship of the Senate and the Praetorians, but when the news of his father's death reached Rome, the boy Caesar and Augustus was assassinated in his mother's arms by the Praetorians.[31]

The two Byzantine authors Zosimus and Zonaras followed the first part of Victor's version in defending the innocent Decius. Zosimus was favourable to Decius, a fellow pagan, who was the only one worthy of rank, and was opposed to the Arab origin of the two emperors. He praised the soldiers' raising of Decius to the throne, considering him superior to Philip in political skill and military experience.[32] Zonaras also followed the same version of the confrontation between Philip and Decius at Verona.[33] These two Greek writers, however, differ from their Latin counterparts in having both emperors, father and son, killed at Verona, fighting in the ranks.[34]

Most modern authors, in their accounts of the death of Philip, follow the traditional version, and see him as having been killed at Verona. They echo the litany of the reluctance of Decius to take the throne, his loyalty and his intention to give up the purple. They state that Philip, in spite of ill health, fought and was defeated and killed in Verona, and his young son killed in Rome.[35]

To both ancient and some modern historians, Decius was a hero and an excellent emperor. But heroes are not supposed to usurp and engineer their illegal election to the purple, so the story of his loyalty, of the letter he wrote to Philip and of his reluctance to assume the purple, are pure fantasy,[36] a fabrication to hide his heinous deeds.

Victor's account of Philip's death has persisted unchallenged for sixteen centuries, until Sloboden Dusanic, a Yugoslav scholar, revised the accepted version in 1976, on the basis of a previously unknown fragment in the Chronique Historique of John of Antioch.[37] This Byzantine historian of the late sixth or early seventh century, relates that there were two successive expeditions against the Goths, the first commanded by Decius in late 248 and the second by Philip in 249,[38] after the millennium celebration.

According to John of Antioch, Philip sent Decius to suppress the revolt of Marinus Pacatianus, who had been declared emperor by the soldiers and had issued coins in Viminacium in his own name. But the revolt evaporated and Pacatianus was assassinated by the very soldiers who had elevated him.[39] The revolt over, Decius made it his mission to fight the Gothic invasions in Moesia and Thrace, but failing in this was discharged from the army and returned to Rome.[40] Many of the defeated soldiers went over to Ostrogtha, the king of the Goths, who received them gladly. Meanwhile, the Carpi and others crossed the Danube and Ostrogatha with 30,000 warriors and 3,000 Carpi, plundered Moesia. Marcianpolis was besieged for a second time.

The second expedition was undertaken by Philip in the spring of 249, after Decius' failure to check the Gothic invasion. Philip successfully repulsed the Goths and threw them back beyond the Danube. He then went to Thrace to prepare for his passage with the army across the Bosphorus.[41] His intention was to move east and confront the usurper Jotapianus in North Syria and Cappadocia, put down the riots in Alexandria and repulse the Persian invasion of Armenia. He marched towards Byzantium and, coming to Perinthus, at the point of passing into Asia,

CHAPTER EIGHT

Philip learned of the usurpation of Decius. It was announced to him that civil strife had broken out in Rome orchestrated by Decius' followers who had gained power in Philip's absence. Philip tried in vain to come to an agreement with the Senate: his belief in constitutional government to the very end seems almost pathetic. In John of Antioch we find a trace of the enmity of the Senate towards Philip: they clearly preferred Decius, Consul and ex-Prefect of the city. Philip sent his agents to calm the insurrection, but when they arrived in Rome they betrayed him. Flattered and bribed by the people and the Senate, they renounced Philip and declared Decius emperor, as did the Romans. Dacia rallied to Decius, while Moesia was loyal to Philip, where the mint continued to issue coins in his name.

A civil war began, in which the Oriental Greek cities with their long-standing rivalries took opposing sides. Thessalonica, the rival of Borea, sided with Decius. The two armies met at Borea and in the ensuring battle, Philip's army was defeated.[42] Dusanic denies that there was a military confrontation between Philip and Decius, but Prickartz concludes that a battle must have occurred on the basis that both the Latin and Byzantine traditions are agreed on the subject.[43]

Defeated in one encounter, Philip was determined to continue the fight. But in September 249, he was assassinated at Borea by the agents of Decius who had daggers hidden under their clothes. Their identity is not known, though they were apparently civilians.[44] In Rome, Philip the younger was assassinated near the camp of the Praetorians, as he left the Palatine palace.[45]

Indications that confirm the account of John of Antioch and the second Danubian campaign are coins which were to be the last of Philip's reign, the 'Fortuna Redux'. They were issued on his departure for the expedition to wish him a happy return to Rome. Coins struck at Antioch in the period bear the legend 'Liberalities Augg III', which signified a donation in the name of the young Philip before the emperor left Rome. Other coins of Antioch have 'Consul IV', probably in anticipation of his fourth consulate, which was not to be. It was a way in which Antioch, anticipating his passage through the city on his way to Syria, could demonstrate its allegiance to Philip in his hour of need. There is no indication of the presence of Julius Priscus in Antioch in 249. Both the coins of 'Fortuna Redux' in Rome and the coins of Antioch signify the absence of the emperor from Rome, for in Antioch, the presence of the emperor was a prerequisite for the functioning of the mint.[46]

The version of John of Antioch, whom Prickartz considers one of the best Byzantine historians, is accepted by Prickartz and York, but many historians such as Stien, de Blois and Loriot have ignored it. Potter dismisses the account as useless. Pohlsander attributes the version to the hostility of John of Antioch to Decius, the enemy of God. Philip was subjected to a *damatio memoriae* and the names of the Philippi were erased from a number of inscriptions.[47]

Philip's death is mentioned in the XIII Sibylline oracle: '...and then, moreover, the high minded one, with his mighty son, will fall by treachery because of the presbyter king.' Here, the murder of Philip and his son by the agents of Decius are attributed to his Christian faith and the influence of Origen, the 'presbyter king'.[48]

This brief, and by no means exhaustive, study shows that Philip the Arab cannot be dismissed merely as one of a series of soldier emperors during the mid-third century crisis, worthy of no more than a few lines in a history book. His accession to the throne was the first living symbol of the unity of the occidental and oriental halves of the Roman Empire, a unity much sought after since Augustus inherited

CHAPTER EIGHT

the conquests of Pompey and Caesar. However, the importance of his brief reign was not merely symbolic, for he brought back to the empire moderation and tolerance, and above all the return of constitutional government. In the words of Nicagoras, 'He liberated Romans from fear. . . The liberty to think and speak has been destroyed and everyone trembled at his own shadow, from this fear he released and freed the souls of all men, restoring to them their liberty whole and entire.'

The curtain then falls on the Arab dynasty, for while a succession of barbarians from the West were to become Roman emperors, no Arab would again aspire to the throne of Rome.

Philip was only 45 years old in September 249, and had been emperor for five years, five months and twenty-nine days. The only fitting epitaph for him is that on his death, the repose which be brought to the Roman world was ended.[49]

EPILOGUE

QUINTUS DECIUS (249-252) seized power after he had killed Philip and his son, and immediately sent edicts for the persecution and killing of the Christians.[1] According to Eusebius, 'His hatred for this prince [Philip]' made him 'persecute our religion.'[2] His hatred and victimisation of Philip resulted in a damnatio memoriae,[3] and the names of the Philippi were erased from many inscriptions. This is confirmed by the Sibyl, written in 253, four years after the murder of Philip; 'But at once, robberies and murders of the faithful there will be suddenly, because of the former king.'[4]

Many stories and legends arose from the persecution, of which the Seven Sleepers of Ephesus was the most popular. It circulated by word of mouth from the third century onwards. It is a tale of Christian youths who, in order to avoid persecution, enter a cave, fall asleep for a long period, and awake in a more enlightened age. The period of their sleep differs from version to version. The story was written down in about the sixth century AD by a Syraic Christian, Simeon Metaphrates, who recorded that the youths were seven in number, that they went to sleep in the reign of the emperor Decius, known for his violent persecution of Christians, and that they awoke in the reign of Theodosius who reigned from 408-456.[5]

Gibbon, in *Decline and Fall of the Roman Empire*, tells the story of the seven Christian youths of Ephesus who left the town and hid themselves in a cave nearby. They fell asleep for some generations or centuries. When the wall sealing the cave was demolished, the youths awoke, thinking they were still in the same world as when they fell asleep. When one of them went to town for provisions, he found the whole world had changed; the Christian religion was fashionable, in fact it was the state religion.[6] The event attracted great attention. The great ones of the land visited the cave and verified the tale by questioning the youths. An inscription was probably placed in the mouth of the cave. In the ninth century, the Khalifa el-Wathiq (AD 842-846) sent an expedition to identify and examine the locality.

But the story is best told in the Quran (Sura al-Kahf). The unbelieving Quraysh were in the habit of putting questions to the Prophet, often based on stories from the Christians and Jews, which they thought the Prophet would be unable to answer. One such question was about the legend of the Seven Sleepers of Ephesus. The Prophet not only told the main story of the youths falling asleep in such faith and trust of Allah, but he also pointed out the variations that were current and rebuked them for disputing such details.[7] Most importantly, he treated the story as a parable of the spiritual lessons of the highest value.[8]

In later times there was controversy over some of the details; whether the number of sleepers was three, five or seven, and as to the exact length of time in the cave. Perhaps this latter point is best left to the Quran – 'Allah knows best how long they stayed.'[9]

The violence of Decius' persecution was far-reaching, in contrast to former Roman emperors who had limited the scope of their attacks. Maximinus reacted to the tolerance shown by Alexander Severus to the Christians with hostility. In AD 235 he deported Pontainus, bishop of Rome, to Sardinia. Origen in Caesarea (Palestine) felt the threat to his safety, because of his relation with the imperial mother Mamaea.[10] Before this, Marcus Aurelius and Septimius Severus had initiated limited bouts of Christian persecution, but with Decius it was a violent systematic persecution all over the empire. The edict he sent in 249, immediately after killing the Philippi, ordered all of his subjects to sacrifice to the pagan gods and he required everyone to obtain a certificate, attesting to the performance of the sacrifice, indicating the exact date it had been made. This action was unprecedented and was motivated purely by Decius' hatred of Philip.[11]

The suffering lasted for a year and there were many martyrs. Babylas in Antioch, Fabian in Rome, and Nestor in Pamphylia (all in January 250) and Pionius in Smyrna (March 250), were but a few.

Dionysius, bishop of Alexandria, wrote that the news of Decius' edict reached Egypt shortly after Philip's death, between September and November 249.[12] The Egyptian certificates (libelli) were particularly searching and demanding. They required that the appellants sacrifice before the superintending officials and must include the signatures of those who witnessed the sacrifice and possibly that of an additional observer. The sacrificant had to testify to his loyalty to the ancestral gods, and had to consume sacrificial food and drink.[13] He was then asked whom he worshipped and asked to offer sacrifice to some acceptable divinity. Those who fraudulently obtained libelli without sacrifice faced penance.

Cyprian wrote that on the day by which sacrifice had to be offered, Christians filled the Capitolium at Carthage in such numbers that the authorities were asked to allow more time. If people did not appear, they might be subject to loss of property. If they refused to sacrifice, they could be tried by laws pertaining to civil disobedience.[14] Lapsed Christians, to demonstrate their pagan piety, sacrificed lambs in the temple of Nemesis, poured libations, and partook of the victims in honour of the ancestral gods. For those who shied from the gods, it was possible to sacrifice to the emperor instead. Those who fulfilled the requirements were called 'libellatici' and 'sacrificati'.[15]

Decius, whose name points to a Dacian origin, was born in Sirmium. His failure as emperor suggest that he was not a man of great personal ability, but a man full of envy, jealousy and hatred. He was not satisfied with the murder of Philip, and with building a story to hide his treachery, but he carried his hatred for his predecessor beyond the grave and extended it through the empire.

The theory was current among Christians that Decius was a forerunner of the Anti-Christ,[16] but it is interesting to note that Decius is known in Arabic literature as 'Daqyanus', a name that stands as a symbol of injustice and oppression, and also of things old-fashioned and out of date.[17] The ways of men are curious. One can only conjecture that Arab writers by naming his thus, after more than a thousand years, were in a way avenging Philip, their fellow Arab and vindicating his death.

NOTES

ABBREVIATIONS

Caes., Aurelius Victor, *Livre des Césare*
Epit., Aurelius Victor, *Epitomee de Caesaribus*
Amm. Jul., Ammianus Marcelinus, Julianus
E.H., Eusebius, *Ecclesiastical (Church) History*
Brev. Eutropius *Brevariarum*
Brev. Festus Rufus, *Brevariarum*
H.A., *Scriptores Historiae Augustae*
Zos, Ann., Zosimus, *Annals*
Zos, N.H., Zosimus, *New History*
Cod. Just., *Codex Justinianus*
Hauran I, Dentzer (editor) *Hauran I, Recherches Archéologiques sur la Syrie du Sud à l'époque Héllenistique et Romaine*

FOREWORD

1. Loriot, *Nonny*, p.7
2. Swift, pp.275, 276, quotes Nicagoras, *Eis Basilia*
3. Dussaud, pp.56, 58
4. Dussaud, op.cit., p.123, *Christides*, p.317
5. Shahid, pp.9,41

CHAPTER I - DENIGRATION AND PREJUDICE

1. Bowersock, p.123
2. Potter, p.217
3. Op.cit, p.218
4. A.Victor, *Epit.*, 28.4, Pohlsander p.468
5. A.Victor, *Caes.* 28, 2
6. *H.A.* Gord, 29.1

7. York, p.321
8. *Amm. Jul.,* 23, 52
9. *Brev. Festus Rufus,* 22.2
10. *Zos, N.H.* 18.3
11. Prickartz, *la Chute,* p.51
12. *Zos, N.H.,* 1, 23.1, Shahid, p.115
13. Eusebius, *E.H.,* 6,34-39, Orosius, 7, 19-20, Potter, p.216
14. Graf, p.345, cites, *Chr.Pasch,* p.271
15. Peachin, p.331, cites, St.Jerome, *Chron,* p.217 York, p.239, Shahid, notes 21,23, p.98
16. Gibbon, pp.140, 354
17. Bury, p.95, *Amm. Jul.*14.41
18. Lissner, p.272
19. Aube, p.148
20. De Blois, p.148
21. Pohlsander, p.465
22. Macdormet, p.8
23. Grant, p.155
24. Olmstead, pp.260, 261
25. Wells, *Encyclopaedia Americana* (Philip)
26. *Camb. Ant. Hist.,* p.92, P.Petit, p.450
27. Coupet et Frezoulis, p.217

CHAPTER II - ARABS BEYOND ARABIA

1. For Arab presence in the Orient, see Shahid, *Rome and the Arabs,* Ch.1, pp.3-16
2. Dussaud, p.23
3. Shahid, p.4 Jones. note 41, p.455
4. Shahid, p.145
5. Plutarch, p.198
6. Jones, p.455, Shahid, p.4
7. Jones, note 41, p.455
8. Jones, pp.256, 260
9. Sartre, *l'Orient,* p.7, Jones, p.260
10. Jones, p.265
11. Dussaud, p.172
12. Sartre, *l'Orient,* p.253
13. Dussaud, op.cit.
14. Shahid, p.38, Jones, pp.265, 266
15. Jones, pp. 246, 253, 255
16. Jones, op.cit. pp.32, 246, Hengel, pp.13, 15
17. Bowersock, p.14

18. Op.cit., pp12, 17
19. Sartre, *Bostra*, p.50
20. Hitti, p.247, Dussaud, pp.63
21. Starcky, pp.17, 176 (*Hauran I*)
22. Graf, p.396
23. Jones, p.290
24. Bowersock, p.64
25. Starcky, op.cit
26. Graf, p.399
27. Bowersock, p.15
28. Graf, pp.388,389
29. O'Leary, p.83
30. Graf, pp.396, note 22, p.400
31. Shurer, p.562
32. Shurer, op.cit. *Dio* 59.12,2, Strabon 16, 2.18
33. Graf, p.373
34. Jones, p.233
35. Jones, op.cit. p.253
36. Graf, p.373
37. Shurer, note 1, p.561
38. Op.cit, p.564
39. Jones, p.253, Shurer, Ibid
40. Jones, pp.253, 285
41. Op.cit, p.281
42. Ibid
43. Shurer, note 53, p.570, Jones, p.258
44. Milik, p.188 (*Hauran I*)
45. Graf, pp.358, 366, 369, 370
46. Graf, p.358, 359. Satre, *l'Orient*, p.35, Dussaud, p.139
47. Milik, op.cit
48. Sartre, Bostra, note 32, p.68, Graf, pp.357, 38
49. Dussaud, pp.139, 145, 147
50. Rostovtzeff, chp.7 (note 36), Graf, p.37
51. Villeneuve, p.17 (*Hauran I*) Milik, p.184 (*Hauran I*), Graf, Rome, p.361
52. Rostovtzeff, p.271, Dentzer (*Hauran I*), pp.402, 412
53. Milik, p.187 (*Hauran I*)
54. Graf, p.364
55. Sartre, Bostra, p.375
56. Graf, pp.361, 364
57. Villeneuve, pp.116, 117 (*Hauran I*)
58. Graf, note 28, pp.375, 379, 400
59. Dentzer, note 59, p415 (*Hauran I*)
60. Sartre, le Peuplement, p.202 (*Hauran I*)

61. Shahid, p.156
62. Graf, p396, Dussaud, p.158
63. Shahid, p.112
64. Tabari, p.395, Bowersock, pp.131-6, Graf, p.345, Dussaud, pp.132, 133
65. Sartre, *l'Orient*, p.315
66. Graf, pp.358, 380, Milik, p.189 *(Hauran I)*
67. Dussaud, p.133

Chapter III - The Hauran

1. The termination ites or itis was commonly used in the Ptolemaic half of Syria. Trachonitis and Auranitis were not heard of before Roman times, Jones, pp.239, 240
2. Sartre, *l'Orient*, p.320
3. Villeneuve, p.7 *(Hauran I)*
4. Smith, p.627
5. Jones, p.237
6. Villeneuve, p.73 *(Hauran I)*
7. Jones, pp.269, 270
8. Starcky, pp.170, 180 *(Hauran I)*
9. Jones, p.270
10. Sartre, M. *l'Orient*, p.320, Starcky, pp.160, 170 *(Hauran I)*
11. Bowersock, pp.49, 50
12. Graf, note 119, p.373
13. Sartre, M.*l'Orient*, p302, Bowersock, pp251, 282, Dentzer, Dev, p.39 *(Hauran I)*
14. Sartre, Trois, p.48 le Peuplement, p.193, *(Hauran I)* Starcky pp.49, 169, 170, 180 (The Hauran)
15. Sartre, Trois, p.60
16. Starcky, 170, Dentzer, p.73 *(Hauran I)*
17. Bauzou, pp.151. *(Hauran I)*
18. Op.cit., p.154
19. Graf, pp.388, 389, Bauzou, p.158, *(Hauran I)* Rostvotzeff, pp.270, 272
20. Bauzou, p.158 *(Hauran I)*
21. Gentelle, p.57 *(Hauran I)* cites G.Reinfleish, 2DPV XXI, 1. 1898 and J.G.Wetzstein, Berlin, 1884, p.17, Dussaud, p.23
22. Hengel, pp.149, 151, 152
23. Jones, p.248
24. Shahid, pp.11, 153
25. Sartre, *l'Orient*, pp.330, 331
26. Smith, p.629

27. Sartre, le Peuplement, note 2, pp.189, 192 (*Hauran I*)

28. Sartre, *le Peuplement*, p.193 (*Hauran I*), *l'Orient*, pp.342.343
29. Ibid
30. Smith, p.365
31. Sartre, *le Peuplement*, p.195 (*Hauran I*)
32. Sartre, *le Peuplement*, pp.201, 202 (*Hauran I*)
33. Sartre, Villes et villages, p.25, *le Peuplement*, p.199 (*Hauran I*)
34. Sartre, Trois p.48, *le Peuplement,* p.193 *(Hauran I)*
35. Jones, p.257
36. Christides, p.317
37. Smith, 267
38. Jones, p.256
39. Bauzou, p.155 (*Hauran I*)
40. Sartre, *Trois* p.256, 56, *Villes et villages,* p.257
41. Shahid, p.28.32
42. Rostovtzeff, note 35, p.666
43. Smith, pp.361, 624
44. Sartre, le *Monde*, pp.493, 126, 49, Smith, note 3, p.628
45. Sartre, *le Monde,* pp.126, 491
46. Graf, pp.381, 382
47. Op.cit., p.383

CHAPTER IV - WAR AND PREJUDICE

1. Potter, pp.190, 191, *Zos, N.H.*18, note 41, p.21, Loriot, Nony, pp.910
2. A.Victor, *Caes*, 27.8, *Epit*, 24, 1-2, *H.A.* Gord, 29.1, *Zos, N.H.* 1.18, *Amm.*, Jul 23, 5.17, Eutropius, *Commentary*, notes 5-9, (ch.9)
3. Victor, op.cit
4. Hadas, p.131
5. Lissner, p.27
6. Potter, p.192
7. *H.A.*Gord., 28, 3.4
8. York, p.234, de Blois, p.16
9. *Ant. Camb. Hist.*, pp81, 82, 86, de Blois, p.12
10. Bowersock, pp.121, 123
11. *Zos, N.H.*24, 1.17
12. Olmstead, p.254, Grant, p.152
13. *Zos, N.H.*24, 1.17
14. Trout, pp.225-227

15. *H.A.Gord.*, 26, 36, 3-6, Potter, pp.193-195
16. Pink, pp. 99, 100, Sartre, p.166
17. A.Victor, *Caes.*27, 8, *Epit*, 24, 2, Olmstead, pp.24, 254
18. Olmstead, p.253
19. A.Victor, Ibid
20. Hadas, p.131
21. A.Victor, *Caes.*, *H.A.* Gord 201-30
22. *H.A.*Gord. 28, 5-6, 9, *Zos, N.H.*, note 36, p.139
23. Olmstead, p.259, Aube, p140
24. Lissner, p.271
25. A.Victor, *Caes.*, 27.8
26. Eutropius, Brev., 9.2-3
27. *Festus, Rufus, Brev.*, 22.2
28. Oost, *the Death*, note 8, p.107, quoting Maricq
29. Amm., Jul.23, 5.7, 17
30. Orosius, 7, 19.5
31. *Zos, N.H.*, 28, 1, 2-3, Prickartz, *la Chute,* p.56
32. Prickartz, Tradition, p.51
33. Zon. Ann., 12.17, 18-19
34. Ibid
35. Potter, p.203
36. York, p.326, Oost, Death, note 9, p.106, quoting Maricq
37. Potter, p.207
38. Ibid.
39. Grant, p.150, Potter, p.36
40. McDormet B.C., pp.80, Loriot, Potter, p.195

42. B.C.Macdormett, pp.76-80, note 81, p.77, Maricq, pp.306, 308, Guey, p.262, Olmstead, p.255, cites Sprengling, Shahpur, p.363, Oost, *Death*, p.106
43. B.C.Macdormett, op.cit., Girshmann, pp.151, 157, Swift, p.285, Grant, p.150, Guey, p.262
44. Guey, pp.262, 274, Pekari, p.275, Olmstead, p.255, quotes Sprengling, Shahpur, Hogman and Maricq p.120, York, p.236, Prickartz, *la Chute*, p.50
45. The Sibylline Oracle, 13, 17-19, Cited in Swift, p.285 Olmstead pp.256, 257, Oost *Death*, p.106
46. *H.A.* Gord, 31.2, *Camb. Ant. Hist.* p.88
47. Potter, pp.210, 211, Eutropius, *Brev*, 9.2, 3
48. York, p.324
49. Rostovtzeff, p.442
50. Lissner, p.4
51. Brauer, p.4
52. C. Sarre, p.165

53. Porrhyry, *Plotinius*, 3-4, Oost, *Death*, p.107
54. Maricq, quoted by Oost, *Death*, note 10, p.107, Potter, p.210
55. Pohlsander, pp.464, 465
56. Ibid
57. Gibbon, p.35
58. Potter, p.28-210, 211, Sibylline Oracle, 1.88
59. Swift, pp. 284, 285
60. Sprengling, Shahpur, p.363, quoted by Olmstead, p.255, Hogman and Maricq p.210
61. Swift, Ibid
62. De Blois, pp.12, 13
63. Macdormett, pp.76-78
64. York, p.325, note 20, p326,323
65. Bowersock, note 6, p.124
66. Shahid, note 57, p.87
67. *Zos. N.H.*, 19.1
68. Sprengling, Shahpur, p.363, quoted by *Camb. Ant. Hist.*, p.88
69. A.Peachin, p.342
70. Potter, p.38, Zos and Zing, p.90
71. Trout, p.230
72. *Zos. Ann.* 12.19, Potter, p.229
73. Olmstead, p.226
74. Brauer, p.11, Peachin, p.342, Guey, pp.276, 278
75. Prickartz, *la Chute*, p.51, *Eis Basilia*, para 14-15, cited by de Blios, p.141
76. Trout, pp.221-223

CHAPTER V - ARABIA REVISITED

1. *Zos, N.H.*19
2. Trout, p.230
3. Bowersock, pp.121, 122, Peachin, p.333, 334
4. Gawltsowski, *les princes*, p.261
5. Jones, p.28, Potter, p.251
6. Peachin, p.334
7. Bowersock, pp.121, 122, Peachin, pp.333, 334
8. Ibid
9. Jones, p.276,
10. Jones, pp.278, 279
11. *Camb. Ant. Hist.* 12, p.511, Sartre, *l'Orient*, p.493
12. Brauer, p.12
13. Coupet et Frezoulis, p.127
14. op.cit., p.103

15. P.Petit, p.449, Zos and Zing, p.89
16. Amer and Gawlikowski, pp.9, 11, 12
17. Brauer, p.13
18. Oost, Alexandrian p.4, Potter, pp.211, 215
19. *H.A.Gord*, 29.1, Zos N.H. 1.18.2, Zos, Ann. 12.19. Downey, p.253, Amer and Gawlikowski, note 13, p.25
20. Amer and Gawlikowski, p.12
21. Potter, note 116, pp.245, 246
22. *Zos N.H.*, 19.1.12, Potter, p.216
23. *Zos N.H.*, 1.20.2, Potter p.246
24. Zos, 19, note 34, Prickartz, p.10
25. Prickartz, la Chute, p.60
26. Zos, note 38, p.138, Petit, p.449
27. A.Victor, *Caes.*, 28, 10-11, X, Loriot, p.149, De Blois, p.35, Bauer, p.13
28. Grant, p.153, Brauer, p.13
29. Amer and Gawlikowski, pp.12, 13
30. Bauer, p.13
31. A.Victor, Epit, 28, 3, Pohlsander, p.218, Seaby, p.19
32. Bowersock, p.123
33. Shahid, p.371
34. De Blois, p.35
35. Charbonneaux, p.265
36. Stien, "Marcia" Rex 4 2,1930, German Encyclopaedia
37. R.A.G.Carson, p.165
38. De Blois, p.35
39. Charbonneaux, p.258
40. *Zos, N.H.*, 1.19,2
41. Stein, Ibid
42. Ibid
43. Turton, p.174
44. Yaqut, p.466
45. Canard, R.A.,pp281-286
46. York, p.339, Canard, pp.281-287
47. Yaqut, op.cit., p.466
48. Canard, p.283 Catalogue of Greek Coins, pp35, p.281
49. Pal. Exp. Fund, 1897, pp.282-284
50. See on this subject; Canard, op.cit, p.284, Peachin, p334, York, op.cit, p.330, Grouzel, p.549
51. A.Victor, *Caes*, 28.1, Bowersock, p.122
52. Sartre, Villes, p.247
53. Amer and Gowlikowski, p.1
54. Coupet and Frezoulis, pp.103, 114, 122, 127
55. Potter, p.252,

56. Sartre, *l'Orient*, p.341, *Camb. Ant. Hist,* p.80, Graf, p,382
57. Sibylline Oracle, 12; 60-70, 64-73, (trans. and quoted by Potter), Olmstead, p.262
58. Potter, pp.153, 249-250
59. Amer and Gowlikowski, p.1, Trout, p.230, Olmstead, p.259
60. Bauzou, pp.145-151 (*Hauran I*)
61. Olmstead, pp.259, 260
62. Amer and Gowlikowski, pp.5, 9,11,12,15
63. Ibid.
64. Olmstead, p.260, Butler, Arch, quoted by Potter, p.252
65. Balty, p.9
66. Op.cit., p.10
67. Coupet and Frezoulis, pp.103, 114, 125, 128, 145
68. Potter, p.252
69. A.Victor, *Caes*, 28.1.
70. Amer and Gowlikowski, pp.14,15, Potter, p.253
71. Charbonneaux, pp.265, 270, 271
72. Will, pp.27-48, Potter, p.250, Charbonneaux, pp.253-257
73. Charbonneux, p.253
74. Op.cit., p.257, Will, pp.27-48
75. Charbonneaux, p.260
76. Dauphin, A Roman, quotes Dunard, p.335, and Dussaud, pp.295-296
77. Dauphin, *Villages Désertés,* p.61, *paysages antiques*, p.57
78. Dauphin, A Roman, pp 32-33

CHAPTER VI -EMPEROR IN ROME

1. De Blois, p.16
2. York, pp.320,321
3. Legends on Coins
4. The two titles appear on papyrus, Inscriptions and Coins, de Blois, p.16, Petit, p.449
5. *Zos, N.H.*, I, 14.2
6. Gibbon, p.161, *Cod. Just.,* IX, 15, 7, York, p.331
7. A.Victor, *Caes*, 28, 6-8, Aube, p.152
8. York, p.331, Grant,u, p.155
9. Potter, p.139
10. A.Victor, *Caes*.28.1.2, 3
11. Parker, p.156, Prickartz, Tradition, note 44, p.157, Pekari, p.231
12. Callu, p.199, A.Victor, *Caes*, p.28.1
13. Cod. Just. X.53.3, Pekari, pp.280, 281, de Blois, p.41

14. De Blois, pp.31, 32, Pekari, p.281. *Zos, N.H. 20.2*
15. De Blois, p.41
16. Brauer, pp.4, 5
17. Op.cit., pp.4,5,8,10, *Camb. Ant. Hist.*, p.90
18. Parsons, pp.138-141
19. Brauer, p.11, de Blois, p.30
20. *Eis Basilea*, Rostovtzeff, p.454/Charbonneaux, p.265, Brauer, pp.5, de Blois, pp.29.34
22. Parker, p.156, de Blois, p.13, *Camb. Ant. History*, p.151
23. De Blois, p.34
24. Callu, p199
25. Greene, b, pp.283,284
26. De Blois, p.34
27. *Eis Basilea*, Swift, p.278
28. Rostovtzeff, p.451, Prickartz, p.53, Petit, p.480, *Camb. Ant. History*, Vol XII, pp.88, 89
29. De Blois, p.18
30. Swift, p.272
31. Op.cit., p.277
32. Swift, 276
33. Rostovtzeff, p.454, Swift, p.277, De Blois, p.17
34. P. Petit, p.448
35. Swift, p.275
36. Parker, p.157
37. Prickartz, Tradition, p.53
38. Olmstead, p.261
39. Porphyry, Vol.I, pp.15, 27
40. Shahid, p.154
41. De Blois, p.13, *Camb. Ant. Hist.*, p.106, Oost, *Death*, p.106, Lissner, p.270, Loriot and Nony, p.258
42. *Eusb. E.H.*, 6.19
43. Porphyry, 1, pp.3, 20
44. Plotinus, Enead, III, 52, 15, p.33
45. York, p.339, Canard, pp.281-287
46. Maricq, p.345
47. Gibbon, p.167, Gage, p.413
48. Brauer, p.14, Potter, p.238
50. Charbonneaux, p.263
51. Gage, pp.416-417
52. Op.cit., p.35, 421
53. De Blois, p.19
54. Grant, p.154, Brauer, p.3
55. Brauer, p.1, Gibbon, p.167, A.Victor, *Caes*, 28.1
56. Lissener, p.273
57. Brauer, p.4

58. Gibbon, p.167, Brauer, op.cit, Eutropius, 9, 3, A.Victor, *Caes.*, notes, p.149, Charbonneaux, p.264
69. Potter, p.238
60. Ibid
61. Grant, p.154
62. Lissner, p.272
63. Pohlsander, p.465, Gage pp.429-430

CHAPTER VII -THE FIRST CHRISTIAN EMPEROR

1. Hannach, pp.105, 154, 157, Bury, p.95
2. Villeneuve, p.118 (*Hauran I*)
3. Bowersock, p.141, CitesEusebius, commentary on Isiah, 42.11
4. Sartre, *le Peuplement*, p.197 (*Hauran I*)
5. Smith, pp.632, 636, Brauer, p.14
6. Eusebius, *E.H.*, 6.21
7. Op.cit., 6.19
8. Op.cit., 6.20, 6.33
9. Ibid
10. Op.cit, 6.38
11. Grant, p.172, Pohlsander, p.64, quotes, Allard, *Hist.*, p.23
12. York, pp.328, 329, Shahid, p.9, Aube, p.141
13. Crouzel, p.548
14. York, pp.320,328
15. Eusebius, E.H.6.36
16. Op.cit., 6.19
17. Hitti, p.372
18. Loriot, Nony, p.264
19. Eusebius, *Who's who*, *E.H.* p.400
20. Loriot, Nony, p.269, quotes, Grégoire le Thaumaturge, *Remerciement*, pp.150-154, 170-171, 181-183 (trans. Crouzel)
21. Bowersock, pp.125,126
22. Eusebius, *E.H.* 6.36
23. Op.cit., 6.34
24. Shahid, p.75
25. Downy, p.307
26. Petit, *Hist.*, note 15, p.449
27. Aube, p.143, York, p.329
28. P.Orisius, 7.20, 28
29. Aube, p.145, Pohlsander, p.463, Shahid, p.67
30. Shahid, p.84
31. P.Orisius, 7.28

32. York, p.321, Pohlsander, p.216
33. Crouzel, p545
34. Shahid, p.81, Peachin, p.334
35. Parker, p.157
36. Loriot, Nony, p.9
37. York, pp.328, 329, Shahid, p91
38. Aube, pp.149-150
39. Pohlsander, p.467, Zon, Ann., 4.36.5
40. Ibid
41. York, p.323
42. Shahid, note 48, p.84, Charbonneaux, note 1, p.264, *Camb, Ant. Hist.*, note 3, p.95
43. Eutropius, *Brev.* 9.2-3, York, p.324
44. Shahid, p.67
45. De Blois, p.41, Petit p.449
46. Parker, p.157
47. Bowersock, p.127, Downey, pp.306-308, note 40, p.67, Potter, p.267
48. Aube, p.40
49. Pohlsander, pp.163, 464, quotes Grégoire *Les Persécutions dans l'Empire Romain,* pp.9,41,89-91, Daniel Repos, p.37, Smith, p.632, Petit p.449
50. Shahid, Rome, Ch.VI, pp.66,93
51. Smith, p633
52. Potter, p.209
53. Ibn-El-Athir, Al Kamel, vol.1,p184
54. Ibn-Khaldun, *Diwan El-Ibr*, vol.2, pp.206, 207, Yusaf Ali (trans. and comment) the Holy Quran, sura 18, El-Khaf, note 2337
55. Al-Qalqashindi, subn El Asha, vol.5,p.389
56. Aube, pp.141,145, Pohlsander, p467

CHAPTER VIII - SIC TRANSIT GLORIA

1. Trout, p.231
2. Petit, p.449
3. *Zos, N.H.*,1.20, *Hades*, p.132, Lissner, pp.270,271, Brauer, p.13, de Blois, p.18, Potter, p.38
4. Potter, op.cit
5. Trout, p.320
6. Brauer, p.12
7. Lissner, p.244
8. *H.A.*Gord, 26, 1-2, de Blois, p.20

9. Oost, *Alex.*, p.3
10. *Zos, N.H.*,1.20, A.Victor, *Ceas.*, 29,2, Loriot, p.799, *Camb. Ant. Hist.*,p.92
11. Olmstead, p.261,
12. *Zos, N.H.* 1.21
13. Ibid.
14. Ibid.
15. Potter, p.257, Rostovtzeff, p.249, *Camb. Ant. Hist,* p.99, Lissener, p.274
16. Grant, p.154
17. Rostovtzeff, p.249
18. Potter, p.39,248
19. Augé, les Monnies, pp.212,213 (*Hauran I*)
20. Potter, pp.155, 156
21. Op.cit., p.39
22. Parker, p.159, Pohlsander, p.468
23. Oost, *Alex.* pp. 4,5, note 17, p.4, Olmstead, p.262, Euseubius *E.H.* 6, 41, 1-8
24. De Blois, p.20
25. Oost, *Alex.*, pp.4,5
26. Allard, p.4
27. Eusebius *E.H.,* 6.39
28. A.Victor, *Caes.*, 28, 10-11, York, p.332
29. Petit, pp.449,450, *Camb. Ant. Hist,* p.93, Potter, p.255
30. Pohlsander, p.214, Grant, p.156
31. A.Victor, *Caes.*,28,1-3, *Epit,* 28,2-3, Eutropius *Brev.* 9,3,9, Orisius,7.20
32. *Zos, N.H.*,1.21
33. Zon, Ann., 12,19
34. Zos, 22,4, Zon, op.cit.
35. Petit, p.449, Brauer, p.17, Grant, p.156, *Camb. Ant. Hist.*, p.94
36. Prickartz, *Tradition,* p.158, Potter, pp.256, 257
37. Prickartz, *la Chute,* p.60,63, quotes Dusanic, pp.436-7
38. J. of Antioch, *Chronique,* quoted by Prickartz, *la Chute,* p.60.
39. Prickartz, *la Chute,* p.59-60, 63, A. Victor, *Caes.* 29,20, *Zos* 1.20, 2. 12,19,
40. Prickartz, *la Chute,* quotes Jordanes, *Getica,* 90
41. Prickartz, *la Chute,* p.59 quotes J. of Antioch frag. 148, Dusanic, *The End,* p.54
42. Prickartz, *la Chute,* note 50, p.60, pp.63,64, note 74, p.64, *Traditions,* p.54, 56, 57, DUsanic pp.434, 437, Dusanic, pp. 436, 437, A.Victor, *Caes,* 28,10, *Zos N.H.,* 1,22

43. York, p.322, Eutropius *Brev*, 9,3, A.Victor, *Caes*, 28, 10, *Epit*, 28,2, Orisius, 7, 20, 4
44. Pohlsander, p.226, York, p.332, quote *Fragmenta Historicorum graecoaum*, IV, pp.599-598, Prickartz, *la Chute*, pp.51, 54, quotes Dusanic
45. A.Victor *Caes*, 28, 10-11, *Epit*, 28, 2-3, Pohlsander, p.220
46. Prickartz, *la Chute*, pp.59, 60, *Traditions*, p.57, cites Mallingly p.109
47. Potter, p.256, Prickhartz, *la Chute* quotes Pohlsander notes, 12, 13, p.53,
48. Pohlsander, p.220, York, p.329
49. Bowersock, p.127

CHAPTER IX - Epilogue

1. Orisius, 7.21
2. Aube, p.43
3. Crouzel, p.545, Potter, pp.143,268
4. XIII Sibylline Oracle, 80, York, p.329
5. Yusuf Ali, (trans. and Comment.) of the Holy Quran, Surah 18, Al Kahaf, note 2337
6. Gibbon, ch.33
7. Surq Al-Kahf, 18.22
8. Yusuf Ali, op.cit., El'Kahf, note 2335
9. Sura, Al Khaf, 18.26
10. *Camb. Ant. Hist.*, p.75
11. Potter, p.261
12. Euseb., E.H., 6.41, 9-10
13. Potter, p.263
14. Op.cit., pp.263, 264
15. Op.cit., note 187, p.265,264
16. Op.cit., p.60
17. Yusuf Ali, op.cit., Al Kahaf, Sara 18, note 2337

MAIN SOURCES

Ammianus Marcellinus, trans. John C.Rolfe (Harvard University Press) London, 1972
Aurelius Victor, *de Caesaribus*, trans. by H.W.Bird, Liverpool University Press, Epitome de Caesaribus ed. F.P. Teubner, Leipzig 1911 (trad. J.E.Bernard)
Carson, R.A.C., *Coins of Greece and Rome* (2nd revised edition), London
Corpus inscriptionum Latinarum
The Digest of Justinian, trans. P.Kreuger, and A.Watson, Philadelphia,1985
Eusebius, *History of the Church*, G.A.Williamson, London, 1989
Eutropius, *Breviarium*, trans. H.W.Bird, Liverpool, 1993
Festus Ruffus, *Abrégé des hauts faits de peuple Romain (Brevariarum)* trad. Arnaud Lindet, Paris
Homer, *The Illiad*, trans. A.J.Murray, vol.I, London, 1978
Hauran I, *Recherches Archéologiques sur la Syrie du Sud à l'Epoque Hellenistique et Romaine;* ed. J.M.Dentzer, CNRS, Paris, 1985
Inscriptiones Latinae Selectae, ed. H.Dessau, vol.I, Zurich, 1974
John of Antioch, *Fragmenta Historicum Graecorum*, IV, ed. C.Muller, Paris, 1851
Orosius, *The Seven Books of History against the Pagans,* trans. Roy. J. Deferrari, Washington, 1965
Plotin, *Ennéads*, ed. E.Berliner, vol 3, Paris, 1981
Scriptores Historiae Augustae, trans. D.Magri, (the three Gordians) vol.2, London, 1924
Syllage Numorum Graecorum, vol.IV, London, 1971
Zonaras, *Epitome Historicum*, ed. L.Dindorf, Vol III
Zosimus, *New History*, trans. R.R.Ridley, Sidney 1928
Al-Asad, Naser Eddine, *N'ashat al-shîr Al-Jahille*, Amman, 1999 (Arabic)

Allard, Paul, *Histoire des persécutions pendant la première moitié du 3ème siècle,* Paris 1984

Al-Tabari, *Tarikh El-Umum,* vol.2, Beirut 1968 (Arabic)

Al-Qalqashandi, *Subh El-Asha,* vol.5, Cairo, 1915 (Arabic)

Amer G. Gawlikowski "Le sanctuaire impérial de Philippopolis" dans *Damaszener Mitteilungen* 2, 1985, p.1-15

Augé, Christian, Les monnaies de fouilles de Si et la circulation monétaire antique dans le Hauran, *Hauran I,* ed.Dentzer

Babelon, *Jean Impératrices syriennes,* Paris 1957

Balty, J.C., "Un portrait de Shanba-Philippopolis et l'iconographie de Philippe l'Arabe", *Publications de l'Institut historique-qrchéologique néerlandais de Stamboul,* LXVII, 1990

Bauzou Thomas, Les voies de communication dans le Hauran à l'époque romaine, *Hauran I,* ed. Dentzer

Bowersock, G.W., *Roman Arabia,* London 1994

Brauer G.C., *The Age of the Solider Emperors, Imperial Rome, AD 244-284,* New Jersey, USA 1975

Bury, J.B, *History of the later Roman Empire,* vol.I New York, 1958

Canard, M. "L'empereur Philippe l'Arabe fut-il un des constructeurs du temple du Jupiter Damascénien, future grande mosquée de damas?", *Revue Africain,* 89, 1945

Charbonneaux, J., "Aiôn et Philippe l'Arabe", *MEFR* 72, 1960

Christides, V., "Arabs as "barbaroi" before the rise of Islam", *Balkan Studies,* vol.10, 1969

Cook, S.A., Alcock, F.E., Charlesworth, M.P., Baynes, N.H., *The Cambridge Ancient History,* vol. XII, The imperial crisis and recovery AD 193-324, Cambridge, 1965

Crouzel, H., "Le chiristianisme de l'empereur Philippe l'Arabe", *Gregorianum,* vol.56, 1975, p.545-550

Coupel,P., Frezoulis E., *Le théatre de Philippopolis en Arabie,* (Inst. Français d'Archéologie Beirut) Paris, 1956

Daniel-Repos, *The Church of Apostles and Martyrs,* New York, 1960

Dauphin, C., "A Roman Mosaic Pavement from Nablus", *Israel Exploration Journal.*29, 1979,

- "Pasages antiques du Golan". *Archéologia,* No.297, January 1994

De Blois, L., "The Church of the Emperor Philip the Arabian", *Talanta* vol. X-XI, Amsterdam, 1978,1979

Dentzer, J-M, "Developpement et culture de la Syrie du Sud dans la période préprovinciale", *Hauran I,* ed. Dentzer

Dawney,G., *A History of Antioch in Syria,* Princeton Un. Press, 1974

Dussaud, R., *La pénétration des Arabes en Syrie avant l'Islam,* Paris 1959

"Eis Basiléa" "An anonymous oration in the corpus of Aelius Aristides XXXV", Berlin 1898 (pp.253-264), translated by Rostovtzeff, in *A social and Economic History of the Roman Empire,* Oxford, 1957 (pp.451-452),

Swift, L., "The anonymous Encomium of Philip", *Greek Roman and Byzantine studies,* vol.7, No.3, 1966, (pp.267-289)

Frezoulis, E., "Du village à la ville, problèmes de l'urbanisation dans la Syrie hellénistique et romaine", *Actes du coll. de Strasbourg Sociétés urbaines, sociétés rurales,* Nov.1985 (ed) E.Frezoulis

Gage,J.I., "Recherches sur les jeux séculaires", *Revue des études latines,* 11,1933, p.400-435

Gawlksowski, M., *les princes de Palmyre,* Syria, LX11

Gentelle, Pierre, "Eléments pour une histoire des paysages et du peuplement du Djebel Hauran septentrional", *Hauran I* (ed) Dentzer

Gibbon, E., *Decline and Fall of the Roman Empire,* Vol I, N.York

Grant, M., *The Roman Emperors, A biographical guide to the rulers of imperial Rome 31 B.C.-A.D.476,* London, 1985

Graf, D.F. "Rome and the Saracens: Reassessing the nomadic menace, l'Arabie préislamique et son environnement historique et culturel", *Actes du colloque de Strasbourg 24-27 Juin 1987* ed. T. Fahd, Leiden, 1989

Greene, B., *God of a hundred names,* London, 1966

Ghirshman, R., *l'Iran des origines à l'Islam,* Paris 1951

Guey, J., *Autour des Res Gestae Divi Saporis:1-Deniers d'or de comptes anciens,* Syria, vol. XXXVIII, 1961

Hacquard,G., *Guide Romain antique*

Hadas, M., *A history of Rome,* London 1958

Harnack, *Expansion of Christianity in the First Three Centuries,* New York, 1908

Hengel, *The influence of Hellenistic civilization in Palestine down to the Maccabean period, studies of the 4th and 3rd centuries BC* (ed) E.Stone and D.Satram, 1980

Honnegman,E., and Maricq, A. *Recherches sur les Gestae dive Saporis,* acad. Roy.Belge, vol.XLVII, Brussels 1953)

Ibn al-Althir, *El-Kamel,* vol. I, Beirut 1983

Ibn Khaldun, *Diwan el Ibr,* vol.2 Beirut, 1971 (Arabic)

Jones, A.H., *Cities of the East Roman Empire* (2nd ed) Oxford, 1970

Kiang D., "The Iconography of Philip the Arab", *American Journal of Archeology,* 85, 1981

Lehman, I.F.W., *Kaisar Gordian III,* Berlin, 1911
Lissner, I., *The Caesars, Might and Madness,* trans. J.Maxwell, Brownjohn, New York 1958
Loriot, X., *Nony Daniel, La crise de l'empire romain,* 235-285, Paris 1997
Le Strange, G., *Palestine under the Moslems,* London, 1890
MacAdam, H.I., "Studies in the History of the Roman Province of Arabia", *Bar International,* series, 295, Oxford 1986
Macdermot, B.C., "Roman Emperors in the Sassanian reliefs", *Journal of Roman studies,* 44,1954
Maricq, A., "Res Gestae dive Saporis", *Syria,* 35,1958
Milik, J.I., Epigraphie Safaitique, *Hauran I,* ed. Dentzer
Mommsen, *Histoire Romaine,* livres V,VI, (trad) Alexandre, Cognat et Toutain, Paris, 1985
Okamura, L., "Western legions in Baalbeck, Lebanon:colonial coins (A.D.244-247 of the Philippi", *Historia* 37,1,1988
O'Leary, Arabia before Mohammed, London 1927
Olmstead, A.T., The Mid-third century of the Christian era", *Classical Philology,* vol.37,1942
Oost, S.I., "The Death of the Emperor Gordian III", *Classical Philology,* vol. LIII,1958
- "The Alexandrian Seditions under Philip and Galienus", *Classical Philology,* vol.56, No.1, Jan.1961
Parker, H.M.D., *A History of the Roman World, AD138 to 337,* Northampton University, 1958
Parsons, P.J., "Philippus Arabs and Egypt", *Journal of Roman Studies,*57,1967,p.134-141
Peachin, M., "Philip's progress", *Historia* 40,1991
Pekari, T., "Autour des Res Gestae Divi Saporis:2-1e 'tribut' aux Perses et les finances de Philippe l'Arabe", *Syria,* vol. XXXVIII, 1961
Petersen, L., *Prosopographia Imperii Romani, saec.I-II-III, Pars IV,* Fasc.3, Berlin
Petit, P., *Histoire générale de l'empire romain,* Paris 1974
Pink, K., "Antioch or Viminacium? A contribution to the History of Gordian III and Philip I", *Numismatic Chronicle,* 5e série, 15,1935
Pohlsander, H.A., "Philip the Arab and Christianity", *Historia,* 29/4, Wiesbaden, 1980
- "Did Decius kill the Philippi?", *Historia,* 31,1982
Potter, D.S., *Prophecy and History in the Crisis of the Roman Empire,* Oxford, 1990
Porphyry, *The Life of Plotinus* (trans), A.H. Armstrong, London 1966
Prickartz, C., "La chute de Philippe l'Arabe (244-249 p.C.n.)

Les Etudes Classiques, vol. LXI, 1993
- "Histoire romaine et tradition byzantine. Le cas du régne de Philippe l'Arabe", G/Braine, J.M.Cauchies (dir.), *La critique historique à l'épreuve,* Liber discipulorum Jacques Paquet, Publications des Facultés universitaires Saint-Louis, Bruxelles, 1989

Plutarch, *Fall of the Roman Republic* (Pompey), (trans) Rex Warner 1981

Remondon, R., *La crise de l'empire romain, de Marc Aurèle à Anastase,* Paris, 1970 (PUF, Nouvelle Clio)

Rostovtzeff, M., *The social and economic history of the Roman empire,* Oxford, vol.I, Oxford 1957

Sarre, Chris, *Chronique des empereurs romains,* trans. Casterman, London 1995

Sartre, M., *L'Orient romain, Provinces et sociétés provinciales en Méditerranée d'Auguste aux Sévères (31 avant J.C.-235 après J.C),* Le Seuil, Paris 1991
- *Bostra, des origines à l'Islam,* Paris, 1985
- *Trois études sur l'Arabie romaine et byzantine,* Bruxelles, 1982
- "Tribus et clans dans le Hawrân antique", dans Syria,59, 1982
Le peuplement et le développement du Hauran antique à la lumière des inscriptions grecques et latines, *Hauran I* (ed) Dentzer
"Villes et villages du Hauran du ler au IV siècle", *actes du Coll. de Strasbourg, Sociétés urbaines sociétés rurales,* Nov.1985 ed. E.Frézoulis

Seaby, H.A., *Roman silver coins,* vol.IV, Gordian III to Postumius, London 1971

Shahid, Irfan, *Rome and the Arabs,* Aprolegomenon, Washington

Shurer, *The History of the Jewish people in the age of Jesus Christ*

Smith, G.A. *The historical geography of the Holy land,* London 1897

Starcky, Jean, "Les inscriptions nabatéennes et l'histoire de la syrie du Sud et du Nord de la Jornanie", *Hauran I* (ed) Dentzer

Stein, A., "Marcia Otacilia Severa", *R.E.,*XIV,2,1930
- "Iulius Philippus", *R.E.,*X,1,1918

Stone, M.E. and **Satram, D.,** *Emerging Judaism, in studies on the 3rd and 4th cent. BC,* Fortren Press, Mineapolis

Trout, D.E., "Victoria Redux and the First Year of the Reign of Philip the Arab", *Chiron* 19,1989

Villeneuve, François, "L'économie rurale et la vie des campagnes dans le Hauran antique (1er siècle avant J.C.-VIè siècle après J.C.)", *Hauran I* , ed. Dentzer

Wood, S., "The Bust of Philip the Arab in the Vatican:a case for the Defense", *American Journal of Archeology,* 86,1982
Wells, Colin,M., "Philip", E*ncyclopaedia Americana*
Will, Ernest, Une nouvelle mosaique de Chahba, Philippopolis *AAS3* (1953)
Yusuf Ali, *Translation and commentary of the Qu'ran* (2nd ed) American Trust company, U.S.A., 1977
Yaqut, Mujem *El-Buldan,* vol.9, Beirut 1968 (Arabic)
York, J.M. "The image of Philip the Arab", *Historia,* 21, 1972

Printed in the United Kingdom
by Lightning Source UK Ltd.
571